Blueprint ONE

Workbook

Brian Abbs
Ingrid Freebairn

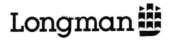

Contents

Unit 1

GRAMMAR: possessive adjectives/
genitive s

3 Chris

4 Jorge

1 Adam

2 Laura

5 Sarah

1 Ask and answer the questions.

1 *What's his name?*
  His name's Adam.

2 *What's her name?*
  Her name's Laura

3 *What's her name?*
  Her name Chris

4 *What's his name?*
  His name's Jorge

5 *What's her name?*
  Her name Sarah

2 Ask questions.

1 Adam/father
  What's his father's name?

2 Laura/sister
  What's her sister's name?

3 Adam/mother
  What's his mother name?

4 Laura/brother
  What's her brother name?

5 you/friend
  What's name my friend?

3 Complete the blanks.

I	my
you	your
he	his
she	she's
it	its

GRAMMAR: verb *to be*

4 Write the full forms.

1 I'm Laura.
  I am Laura.

2 He's my brother.
  He is my brother

3 She's my sister.
  She is my sister

4 It's your ticket.
  It is your ticket

5 What's your book called?
  What is your book called?

1

Unit 2

JUNE

Sun	M	T	W	T	F	Sat
			① Ben	2	3	4
⑤ Juliet	6	7	8	9	10	11
12	⑬ George	14	15	16	17	18
19	20	21	22	23	24	㉕ Chris
26	27	28	29	㉚ Theresa		

1 Look at the calendar and complete the sentences.

1 It's Ben's birthday on ..*Wednesday*..

2 It's Theresa's birthday on ..*Tuesday*..

3 It's ..*George's*.. birthday on Monday.

4 It's Chris's birthday ..*on Saturday*..

5 It's Juliet's ..*birthday on Sunday*..

COMMUNICATION

2 Ben meets Juliet on Wednesday morning. Complete the conversation using the words and expressions in the box.

this is   Thanks   Hello   on Monday
I'm fine   How do you do   Goodbye

JULIET: ¹ *Hello*.., Ben. How are you?

BEN: ² *I'm fine*.., thanks.

JULIET: Ben, this is my father.   Dad,
            ³ *this is*.. my friend, Ben.

MR JACKSON: How do you do, Ben.

BEN: ⁴ *I'm fine*..,
            Mr Jackson.

JULIET: It's Ben's birthday today.

MR JACKSON: Oh, have a nice day, Ben!

BEN: ⁵ *Thanks*.., Mr Jackson.
            I must go now, Juliet.

JULIET: O.K. ⁶ *see you on Monday*.., Ben.

BEN: Bye! See you ⁷ *Goodbye*..!

WRITING: punctuation

3 Use full stops (.) and CAPITAL letters to write three sentences about Ben and Juliet.

it is ben's birthday on wednesday on wednesday morning he meets juliet jackson and her father it is juliet's birthday on sunday

1 *It is Ben's birthday on Wednesday.*

2 ....

....

3 ....

....

VOCABULARY

4 Complete the groups of words.

Monday	morning	yesterday
Thursday	afternoon	today
Wednesday	evening	tomorrow
Tuesday	night	
Friday		
Saturday		
Sunday		

Unit 3

1 SUSHI BAR

2 KENTUCKY FRIED CHICKEN

3 *Le Bistro* FRENCH CUISINE

4 **The Taj Mahal** The best in Indian food

5 **Zorba's Taverna** With live Greek music every night

6 *THE SMÖRGÅSBORD* *Swedish open sandwiches a speciality*

GRAMMAR: verb *to be*

1 Write short answers about the restaurants.

1 Is it Chinese?

No, it isn't.

2 Is it American?

Yes, it is.

3 Is it French?

....

4 Is it Italian?

....

5 Is it Greek?

....

6 Is it Dutch?

....

VOCABULARY: nationality adjectives

2 Say what language the greetings are.

1 You are in Spain. | Buenos dias.

It's Spanish.

2 You are in Turkey. | Merhaba.

It's Turkey's

3 You are in Italy. | Buon giorno.

It's Italys

4 You are in China. | 你好 (nǐ hǎo)

It's Chinas

5 You are in Greece. | καλημέρα (Kalimera)

It's Greeks

6 You are in the USSR. | Здравствуйте (Zdravstvuytye)

It's USSR's

3

3 Write the nationalities in four groups according to their endings.

Americ- Swed- Portugu-	Span- Brit- Germ-	Japan- Russ-	Ital- Turk-	Chin- Argentin-

-an	-ian	-ish	-ese
American	....	....	....
....	....	....	....
	....	....	....
		....	

COMMUNICATION

4 Read this dialogue.

AKIKO: What's your name?
ANN: My name's Ann Evans.
AKIKO: Are you English?
ANN: No, I'm not.
AKIKO: Where are you from?
ANN: I'm from Cardiff.
AKIKO: Where's Cardiff?
ANN: It's in Wales.
AKIKO: Oh, you're Welsh!
        Do you speak Welsh?
ANN: Yes, I speak English and Welsh.

Write a similar conversation. You meet David Walker. You think he's American but he's Canadian. He's from Toronto, in Canada.

YOU: *What's your name?* ....

DAVID: ....

YOU: ....

DAVID: ....

YOU: ....

DAVID: ....

YOU: ....

DAVID: ....

YOU: ....
        Do you speak French?
DAVID: Yes, I speak English and French.

WRITING

5 Complete the paragraph about David. Then write about Ann in your notebook.

His name's *David Walker* He's .... He's from .... in .... He speaks .... and ....

Unit 4

GRAMMAR: singular/plural

1 Write questions and answers about the objects in the picture.

1 *What's that in English?*
   It's a table.

2 *What's that in English?*
   It's an umbrella.

3 *What are those in English?*
   They're oranges.

4 ....
   ....

5 ....
   ....

6 ....
   ....

7 ....
   ....

GRAMMAR: prepositions

2 Write questions and answers saying where the objects are.

1 oranges
   Where are the oranges?
   They're in the bowl.

2 stamp
   Where's the stamp?
   It's on the envelope.

3 umbrella
   ....
   ....

4 pens
   ....
   ....

5 books
   ....
   ....

6 envelope
   ....
   ....

WRITING

3 Join the parts of the sentence using *and* or a comma (,). Study the examples first.

1 The umbrella/the books are on the chair.

The umbrella and the books are on the chair.

2 The French flag is blue/white/red.

The French flag is blue, white and red.

3 The apples/the oranges are in the bowl.

....

....

4 The Italian flag is red/white/green.

....

....

5 The dictionary/the notebook are Laura's.

....

....

6 John/Karen/Michael are from Leeds.

....

....

VOCABULARY: categories

4 Write the following words in alphabetical order (A-Z) in the correct column.

| apples | chair | white | lamp | drawer |
| oranges | green | desk | yellow | blue |

Colours   **Furniture**

....

....

....

....

Fruit

apples

....

VOCABULARY: colours

1 HTIWE

4 LEWYLO

5 IKNP

3 EDR

6 KCALB   2 ULBE

5 Sort the letters in each box, then write sentences to describe the colours in the photograph.

1 *It's white.* ....

2 *They're blue.* ....

3 ....

4 ....

5 ....

6 ....

6

INTERNATIONAL CLUB
MEMBERSHIP CARD

Name _Miss Silvia Mondi_
Address _c/o Turner,_
12A, Minster Gardens,
York, YO1 2AS,
England

Membership no _51046_

COMMUNICATION

1 Complete the conversation with Silvia.

1 YOU: _What's your name?_
  SILVIA: Silvia Mondi.

2 YOU: ....
  SILVIA: I'm 21.

3 YOU: ....
  SILVIA: From Treviso in Italy.

4 YOU: ....
  SILVIA: No, I'm not. I'm single.

5 YOU: ....
  SILVIA: It's York 87324.

READING AND WRITING

2 Read this paragraph.
Then use the form on the
right to write a similar
paragraph about
Hannelore in your
notebook.

Silvia Mondi is an Italian
student from Treviso. She
is twenty-one years old.
She isn't married. Her
address in Britain is:
c/o Turner, 12A, Minster
Gardens, York, YO1 2AS.

3 You are sending a parcel to Hannelore.
Write her name and address on the label.

VOCABULARY: numbers

4 Write the numbers.

1	_one_	13	....
2	....	30	....
3	....	58	....
4	....	60	....
10	....	75	....
11	....	100	_a hundred_

INTERNATIONAL CLUB
MEMBERSHIP APPLICATION FORM

FIRST NAME _Hannelore_ SURNAME _Beck_
NATIONALITY _Danish_
PLACE OF BIRTH _Copenhagen_
AGE _31_ OCCUPATION _Teacher_
SINGLE [ ] MARRIED [ ] DIVORCED [X]
ADDRESS IN BRITAIN _c/o Barnes, 34, Clevedon Rd,_
Richmond, TW1 2FX, England
TELEPHONE NUMBER _—_

☰ *Listening and speechwork 1–5*

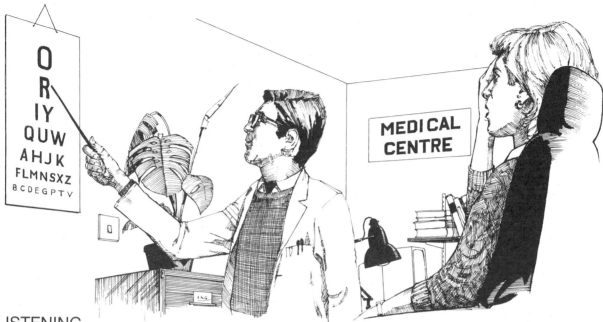

LISTENING

1 Listen and complete the information on the medical card.

MEDICAL CARD

NAME *Anna Ternberg*

ADDRESS ....

....

....

....

TELEPHONE ....

DOCTOR *M. E. Stapley*

2 Listen and circle the letters Anna gets wrong in her eye test.

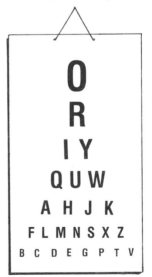

O
R
I Y
Q U W
A H J K
F L M N S X Z
B C D E G P T V

3 Do the hearing test. Circle the word or number you hear.

1 mother   father   (brother)
2 Saturday   Sunday   Monday
3 three   thirteen   thirty
4 grey   yellow   green
5 007   335   339

ORAL EXERCISES

4 Answer the doctor's questions and read the eye test letters on page 8.

5 Respond to the introductions.

T: My name's Adam.
s: *How do you do, Adam*

1 Adam   4 John
2 Chris   5 Mr Burton
3 Anna

6 Correct the numbers.

T: Is that 0 8 double 0 4?
s: *No, it isn't, it's 0 8 double 0 5.*

1 08005   4 0755
2 526–3791   5 13
3 992–4711

7 Listen to a word and ask how to spell it. Then write it in the space below.

T: mother
s: *How do you spell that?*
T: m-o-t-h-e-r

1 *mother* ....

2 ....

3 ....

4 ....

5 ....

STRESS

8 Listen to the word, ask the speaker to repeat it and underline the stressed syllable.

T: yesterday
s: *Can you say that again, please?*
T: yesterday

1 yesterday
2 tomorrow
3 morning
4 afternoon
5 Italy
6 Italian
7 Japan
8 Japanese

PRONUNCIATION

Vowel sounds

/ ɪ / | It's | English. |
/ i: / | He's | Japanese. |

9 Listen and tick the sound you hear.

	/ ɪ /	/ i: /
1	....	......✓......
2	....	....
3	....	....
4	....	....
5	....	....
6	....	....

10 Listen and repeat the words and phrases.

It's English.   This is Chris.
Chris is his name.   Chris is English.
This is Mrs Gibson   What's this in English?

he   we   she
He's Japanese.   She's fourteen.
We speak Chinese.   She's Teresa Green.

Consonant sound

/ dʒ / | Japan | German |

11 Listen and repeat the words and phrases.

George   John   Jan
German   Germany
Japan   Japanese
Algiers   Algerian

Unit 6

THE GOOD TRAVEL COMPANY

Do you like travelling and meeting people?

Can you: ▷ write and type letters?
▷ use a computer?
▷ answer the telephone?
▷ drive a car?
▷ speak a foreign language?

IS THE ANSWER 'YES'?

Write to us today at: THE GOOD TRAVEL COMPANY, 43, Canal Street, London, E12 2BV, England

GRAMMAR: can/can't (ability)

1 Two people see this advertisement and list what they can do. Answer questions about their skills.

	Kate	Richard
write letters	✓	✓
type letters	✓	
use a computer	✓	
answer the telephone	✓	✓
drive a car		✓
speak a foreign language	✓	✓

1 Can they write letters?
  Yes, they can.

2 Can they type letters?
  Kate can but Richard can't.

3 Can they use a computer?
  ....

4 Can they answer the telephone?
  ....

5 Can they drive a car?
  ....

6 Can they speak a foreign language?
  ....

WRITING

2 Use the chart below to write sentences about your abilities in English. Use *and, but* and *or*. Write true sentences.

COUNT	to twenty to a hundred
UNDERSTAND	a popular song the English news on BBC radio
READ	a menu a newspaper
WRITE	a holiday postcard a letter
GREET INTRODUCE	someone someone

1 *I can count to twenty and to a hundred.*
  I can count to twenty but I can't count to a hundred.
  I can't count to twenty or to a hundred.

2 ....
  ....

3 ....
  ....

4 ....
  ....

5 ....
  ....

Unit 7

	Number 1	Number 3	Number 5	Number 7
SURNAME	....	....	....	....
HUSBAND'S NAME	....	*Shadi*	....	*Rob*
WIFE'S NAME	....	....	*Betty*	....
CHILDREN Boys	*John 3*	*Darshan 20* *Surojit 15*	*Mark 22*	*None*
Girls	*None*	*Ranjit 12*	*Jenny 18*	*None*

READING AND WRITING

1 Try this puzzle. Four families live in a street. Use the clues below to write their names in the chart.

1 Mr and Mrs Parry live at Number 1.
2 Mr and Mrs Kildare haven't got any children.
3 Mr Singh's first name is Shadi.
4 Mrs Woodhead is called Betty.
5 Betty's husband's name is Norman.
6 Bill and Helen Parry have a boy called John.
7 Shadi's wife Surinder is a friend of Gina Kildare.

Now check to see if you are right. Look at the bottom of the opposite page.

GRAMMAR: verb *have got*

2 Write a sentence about each family.

1 THE PARRYS: *Mr and Mrs Parry at Number 1 have got one child.*

2 THE SINGHS: ....
....

3 THE WOODHEADS: ....
....

4 THE KILDARES: ....
....

3 Answer questions about the families.

1 How many children have the Woodheads got?
They've got two.

2 How many children have the Kildares got?
They haven't got any.

3 How many brothers has Ranjit got?
....

4 How many sisters has Mark got?
....

5 How many sons have the Singhs got?
....

6 How many daughters have the Parrys got?
....

4 Write the sentences using the full form of *has* or *is* where necessary.

1 Helen's got one son.
Helen has got one son.

2 Helen's son's three.
Helen's son is three.

3 Norman's got a son and a daughter.
....

4 Jenny's got a brother called Mark.
....

5 Surinder's Shadi's wife.
....

6 Who's Gina's husband?
....

VOCABULARY: the family

5 Write the following words in the correct place in the chart.

grandmother mother husband aunt son nephew parent grandfather baby uncle sister brother wife cousin child daughter grandparent father niece

Female	Male	Male and female
		grandparent
wife		
	father	
daughter		
	brother	
niece		
		baby

6 Complete the table with the correct singular or plural form.

Singular	Plural
....	*wives* ....
uncle	....
....	*babies* ....
cousin	....
aunt	....
child	....

	Number 1	Number 3	Number 5	Number 7
SURNAME	Parry	Singh	Woodhead	Kildare
HUSBAND'S NAME	Bill	Shadi	Norman	Rob
WIFE'S NAME	Helen	Surinder	Betty	Gina

12

Unit 8

GRAMMAR: present simple

1 Write questions using *What* or *Where*.

1 (What/you/do)
What do you do ?

2 (Where/you/live)

....

3 (What/your girlfriend/do)

....

4 (Where/she/live)

....

5 (Where/your parents/live)

....

2 Write short answers.

1 Do you live near here?   (No)
No, I don't.

2 Do you like your job?   (Yes)

....

3 Does your brother live here?   (No)

....

4 Do your parents like your friends?   (Yes)

....

5 Does your sister live at home? (Yes)

....

GRAMMAR: prepositions

3 Complete the sentences with *in, on, for, at* or *with*.

1 My mother teaches French ......*in*...... Paris.

2 My husband is a journalist .... the *Evening News.*

3 My brother works .... a farm
.... the country.

4 Jose plays football .... Bayern Munich.

5 Michel lives .... home .... his family.

13

READING

4 Read the text and answer the questions.

ALEX SABELLA

ALEX SABELLA is a footballer. He is Argentinian but he plays football for Sheffield United in England. He is married and lives in Sheffield with his wife, Concepción, and baby daughter. His wife teaches Spanish at an English school in Sheffield. His family live near Buenos Aires. His father is a farmer.

1 What does Alex do?
He's a footballer

2 What nationality is he?

....

3 What team does he play for?

....

4 What does his wife do?

....

5 Where do his family live?

....

6 What does his father do?

....

WRITING

5 In your notebook, write a similar paragraph about Dolena using the notes.

Name:	Dolena Suarez
Job:	nurse
Nationality:	Portuguese
Place of work:	hospital in Birmingham
Husband's name:	Jose - Luis
Husband's job:	waiter in a hotel
Family:	near Oporto
Jobs:	father sells newspapers and magazines
	mother a housewife

Unit 9

Speech bubbles (top):
- Oh! Sorry! Goodbye.
- Really? Why not?
- Why don't you like them?
- Hello. Enjoying the party?

- I don't like parties.
- No, not very much.
- I don't drink, I can't dance and I don't like talking to strangers.

COMMUNICATION

1 Andy meets Clare at a party. Put the sentences from the bubbles in the correct order and write their conversation.

ANDY: *Hello. Enjoying the party?* ....

CLARE: ....

ANDY: ....

CLARE: ....

ANDY: ....

CLARE: ....

....

ANDY: ....

2 Write another party conversation.

| 1 Greet/Give name/Ask name | A: *Hello. I'm Gina. What's your name?* .... |

| 2 Give name/Ask where A is from | B: .... |

| 3 Answer/Ask where B lives | A: .... |

| 4 Answer/Ask what A does | B: .... |

| 5 Answer/Ask if B likes the music | A: .... |

| 6 Answer/Say what music you like | B: .... |

| 7 Ask if B likes dancing | A: .... |

| 8 Say you can't dance | B: .... |

| 9 Say you must go. Say goodbye | A: .... |

| 10 Say goodbye | B: .... |

GRAMMAR: like/object pronouns

JOY: Do you like Jane's dress?

MARIA: It's O.K. but I don't like the colour very much.

JOE: Do you like Kate?

NIGEL: Yes, very much.

JOE: Well, ask her to dance then!

NIGEL: She doesn't like dancing very much and she doesn't like me at all!

MRS SMITH: We like doing household jobs.

MR SMITH: Yes, we both like cooking, cleaning, and shopping very much.

KATE: Really? How interesting!

TOM: Do you like the Smiths?

SALLY: No, not very much. I think they're boring.

TOM: Oh, I like them.

STEVE: It's a good party.

CHRIS: Yes, very good. The music is great.

STEVE: And the food too!

KEVIN: The salad's good.

ALICE: Yes – but cold paella! Ugh! I don't like it at all.

3 Answer the questions about the party.

1 Does Nigel like Kate? — *Yes, he likes her very much.*
2 Does Kate like Nigel? — *No, she doesn't like him at all.*
3 Does Maria like Jane's dress? — *It's O.K. but she doesn't like the colour very much.*
4 Does Alice like the paella? — ....
5 Do the Smiths like cooking? — ....
6 Does Sally like the Smiths? — ....
7 Do Steve and Chris like the party? — ....

WRITING

4 Mats Olsson is Swedish. His English teacher corrects his written English with these symbols:

G = check grammar
P = check punctuation
Sp = check spelling
WO = incorrect word order
∧ = put something here

Rewrite in your notebook the correct form of Mats' letter.

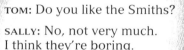

Ostermalmsgatan 68A,
11145 Stockholm,
Sweden
∧

Dear Mr and Mrs Cross,

I am a twenty-year-old male student from (s)weden. I'm studying *P*
P P (e)nglish and (f)rench. I like travelling and I am interested
Sp G in music, (litterature), (the) keep fit(), and politics.   *P*

I can do most household jobs. I can cook and I like
WO gardening. I can (very well) drive a car and I enjoy (to cycle). *G*
I can swim quite well and I like (very much) walking. I love *WO*
children. (Do you have got) many children?   *G*

Last summer I was an 'au pair' for Mrs J. Cooper at
WO Old Street (42,) Cambridge. Please write to her. She can tell
you all about me.
Yours sincerely,
Mats Olsson
∧

Unit 10

GRAMMAR: prepositions

1 Answer the questions about St Lucia using the prepositions *in* and *on* and a point of the compass.

1 Where's Castries?
It's on the west coast of the island

2 Where are the Pitons?
They're in the west of the island

3 Where's Gros Islet?
....

4 Where's Dennery?
....

5 Where's the airport?
....

6 Where's Vieux Fort?
....

GRAMMAR: the article

2 Complete the sentences about St Lucia using *the* or *a/an*.

1 Soufrière is a town on ...*the*... west coast.

2 .... capital of St Lucia is Castries.

3 The airport is in .... south of the island.

4 .... Caribbean Sea is in .... west and .... Atlantic Ocean is in .... east.

5 Rodney Bay has .... beautiful beach.

6 Micoud is .... town on .... east coast.

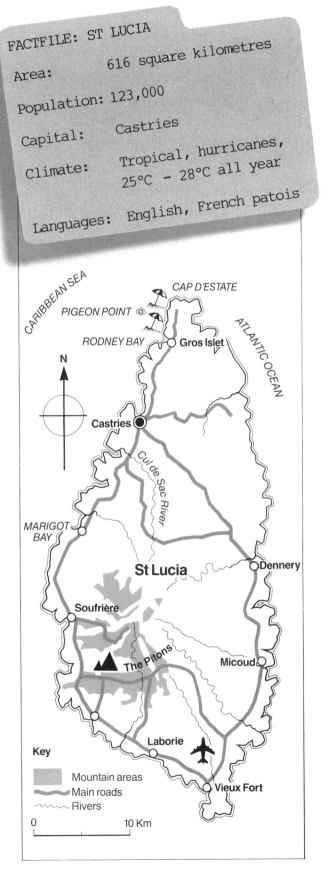

FACTFILE: ST LUCIA

Area: 616 square kilometres

Population: 123,000

Capital: Castries

Climate: Tropical, hurricanes, 25°C – 28°C all year

Languages: English, French patois

COMMUNICATION

3 Complete the interview with questions about St Lucia.

1 Where/you?

MARK: *Where do you come from ?*
TERESA: I come from St Lucia.

2 Where/it?

MARK: ....
TERESA: It's in the Windward Islands.

3 Where/exactly?

MARK: ....
TERESA: They're in the East Caribbean.

4 What/St Lucia/like?

MARK: ....
TERESA: It's beautiful, but very poor.

5 What/famous for?

MARK: ....
TERESA: Its beautiful beaches and its volcanic mountains – the Pitons.

6 What/language?

MARK: ....
TERESA: English is the official language but people also speak French patois.

VOCABULARY:
places/adjectives

4 Match the symbols with the words.

a   b

c   d

e   f

1 art gallery $\boxed{b}$

2 football team $\square$

3 cathedral $\square$

4 mountain $\square$

5 beach $\square$

6 river $\square$

WRITING

5 Look at the chart and write sentences about the towns and cities.

1 *Florence is a beautiful old city in the centre of Italy. It is famous for its museums and art galleries.*

2 ....
....

3 ....
....

4 ....
....

5 ....
....

Place	Description	Location	Famous for
Florence	beautiful old city	centre/ Italy	museums/ art galleries
Munich	big industrial city	south/ Germany	football team
Rio de Janeiro	big tourist port	east coast/ Brazil	beaches/ Sugarloaf Mountain
Cambridge	beautiful old city	east/ England	university
San Francisco	beautiful and interesting city	west coast/ USA	bridge/ cable cars

▦ *Listening and speechwork 6–10*

LISTENING

Woodstock is a small country town. The town council have got a plan for a big new sports centre and want to know if people like it.

1 Listen to some of the interviews and complete the opinion poll questionnaire.

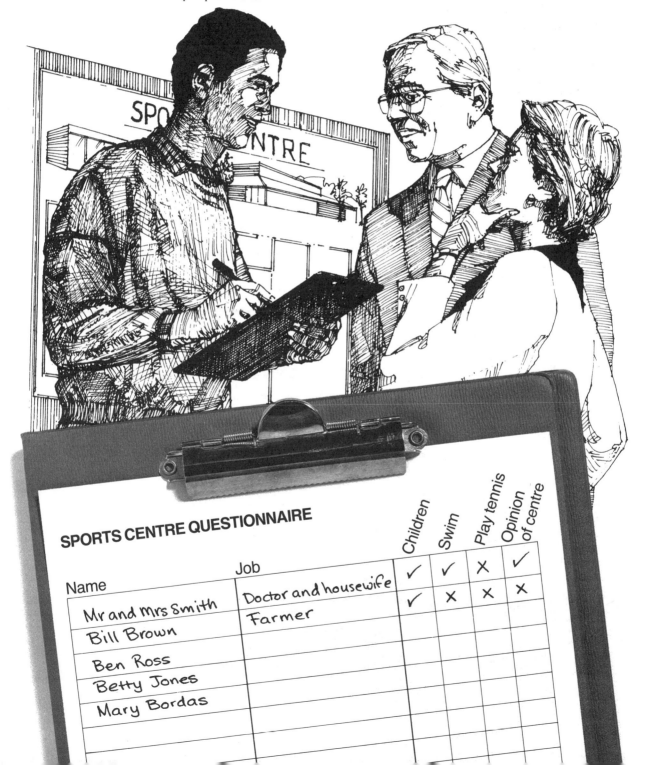

SPORTS CENTRE QUESTIONNAIRE

Name	Job	Children	Swim	Play tennis	Opinion of centre
Mr and Mrs Smith	Doctor and housewife	✓	✓	✗	✓
Bill Brown	Farmer	✓	✗	✗	✗
Ben Ross					
Betty Jones					
Mary Bordas					

ORAL EXERCISES

2 Answer questions about children.

T: Have Mr and Mrs Smith got any children?
S: *Yes, they have.*

1 Mr and Mrs Smith
2 Bill Brown
3 Ben Ross
4 Betty Jones
5 Mary Bordas

3 Use your questionnaire to answer questions about the sports centre.

T: Do Mr and Mrs Smith like the sports centre plan?
S: *Yes, they do.*

1 Mr and Mrs Smith
2 Ben Ross
3 Mary Bordas
4 Bill and Betty

4 Use your questionnaire to say what people can and can't do.

T: What can Mr and Mrs Smith do?
S: *They can swim but they can't play tennis.*

T: What can Bill do?
S: *He can't swim or play tennis.*
T: What can Ben do?
S: *He can swim and play tennis.*

1 Mr and Mrs Smith
2 Bill Brown
3 Ben Ross
4 Betty Jones
5 Mary Bordas

STRESS

5 Listen and underline the stressed syllable.

<u>doc</u>tor	housewife	farmer
teacher	singer	student

6 Use your questionnaire to answer questions about people's jobs.

T: What do you <u>do</u>, Mr Smith?
S: *I'm a doctor. What do <u>you</u> do?*

PRONUNCIATION

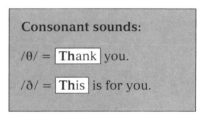

Vowel sounds

/æ/ = Yes, I can.

/ɑ:/ = No, I can't.

7 Listen to the sentences and tick the sound you hear.

	/æ/	/ɑ:/
1	✓	....
2	....	....
3	....	....
4	....	....
5	....	....
6	....	....

Now listen and repeat the sentences.

Consonant sounds:

/θ/ = Thank you.

/ð/ = This is for you.

8 Listen and repeat the words and sentences.

thanks   thank you
this   these   that   those
This is my mother.
This is my brother.
My brother is thirty-three.

Unit 11

1 Write the time of day.

1 10 a.m.   *It's ten o'clock in the morning.*

2 6.30 p.m.   ....
....

3 11 a.m.   ....
....

4 3.15 p.m.   ....
....

5 7.45 a.m.   ....
....

GRAMMAR: present simple/ prepositions

2 Complete the sentences with *do* or *does*.

1 What time ..*does*.. the train leave?

2 What time .... the banks open?

3 What time .... they close?

4 What time .... the plane arrive?

5 What time .... the classes start?

3 Complete the sentences with the correct preposition.

1 It starts ..*at*.. half past six ..*in*.. the evening.

2 The train arrives .... half past ten .... night.

3 The class is from five thirty .... seven .... the evening.

4 What time does it close .... Saturdays?

5 Lunch is .... one o'clock.

6 Is it twenty .... or twenty past ten?

READING

4 Answer questions about Monday night's BBC TV programmes.

6.00 Brookside
Serial story on Mondays and Wednesdays

6.30 Countdown
Quiz game

7.00 News

8.00 Have a nice day
Comedy programme

8.30 Time to travel
Travel programme: Jane and Kevin go to Corfu.

9.00 La Bohème
Opera from Covent Garden

11.00 World at War
Documentary programme

12.00 Film The Black Hole (1985)
Science fiction film about a German scientist

1.55 Close

1 What time is the news?
At seven o'clock.

2 On what days can you watch *Brookside*?
....

3 What's the name of the quiz programme?
....

4 What time does the opera finish?
....

5 What type of programme is *Have a Nice Day*?
....

WRITING

5 Bob Jones likes comedy programmes. He leaves a note for his friend to record a programme on his video recorder.

Tim,
Please record 'Have a nice day'. It starts at 8 p.m. and finishes at 8.30.
Thanks, Bob

You like travel programmes. In your notebook, write a similar note for your partner.

Unit 12

Life of a tennis star

ARANTXA SANCHEZ works six and a half hours a day. She gets up at 8 a.m. and eats a big breakfast. At 9.25 she leaves home and goes to the Barcelona Tennis Club. She plays tennis with her coach, Juan Nunez, from 9.30 to midday. She has lunch from 12 to 2 and then rests for an hour. At 3 p.m. she plays tennis again until half past five and then rests. At 6 p.m. she starts ninety minutes of keep-fit exercises and then goes home. She has dinner at 8.30 p.m. and goes to bed at 10 p.m. 'I have no time for boyfriends,' says Arantxa!

DAILY ROUTINE

- get up
9.25 a.m. - leave home
- arrive at club to play tennis
- lunch
2.00 p.m. - rest
- play tennis
5.30 p.m. - rest
6.00 p.m. - do exercises
- go home
8.30 p.m. - have dinner
- go to bed

READING

1 Read the article and complete the notes about Arantxa Sanchez's daily routine.

GRAMMAR: present simple/ adverbs of frequency

2 Use the information in Exercise 1 to answer the questions.

1 What time does Arantxa get up?
   She gets up at eight o'clock.

2 What time does she start to play tennis in the morning?
   ....

3 What time does she have lunch?
   ....

4 What time does she do her keep-fit exercises?
   ....

5 What time does she go home?
   ....

3 Write questions to complete the interview with Arantxa Sanchez about her daily routine.

YOU: *What time do you get up?*

A.S.: I get up at 8 a.m. and eat a big breakfast.

YOU: What time .... at the Barcelona Tennis Club?

A.S.: I usually arrive at about half past nine.

YOU: What .... in the morning?

A.S.: I play tennis for two and a half hours with my coach.

YOU: What ....

A.S.: His name's Juan Nunez.

YOU: What time ....

A.S.: I have lunch at midday and then rest for an hour.

YOU: What .... after lunch?

A.S.: After lunch I play tennis again.

YOU: What time ....

A.S.: At seven thirty.

Arantxa Sanchez beats Steffi Graf to win the French Open Championship.

4 Write about your own routine. Complete the sentences as you like.

1 always/every morning

I always get up at seven every morning.

2 usually/on Friday evening

....

3 never/on Sunday morning

....

4 often/on Saturday night

....

5 sometimes/at the weekend

....

WRITING

5 Join each pair of sentences with *and* or *but* to write a paragraph about a week's routine.

1 I get up at seven thirty. I usually leave the house at eight thirty.
2 I start work at nine. I work until half past twelve.
3 I always have lunch at work. I don't have a big lunch.
4 In the evening I usually watch TV. I go to bed at about eleven.
5 On Saturday I do housework all day. I always go out in the evening.

I get up at seven thirty and (1) usually leave the house at eight thirty.

....

....

....

....

....

....

....

....

....

Unit 13

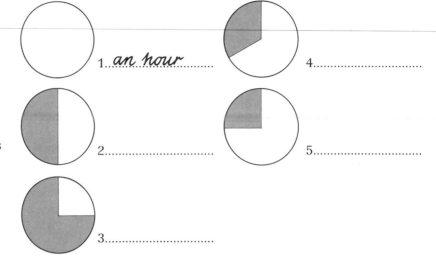

1 *an hour*

2 ....

3 ....

4 ....

5 ....

VOCABULARY: time/transport

1 Write the correct periods of time.

a quarter of an hour
half an hour
forty minutes
three quarters of an hour
an hour

WRITING

2 Look at the chart and write three sentences about each person.

Name	Job	Transport	Leaves home	Arrives at work
1 Terry	engineer		7.30	8.15
2 Jenny	secretary		7.45	8.45
3 William	teacher		8.20	8.40
4 Helen	solicitor		8.00	8.30
5 Harry	accountant		9.10	9.30

1 *Terry is an engineer. He goes to work by bus.*
It takes him three quarters of an hour.

2 ....

....

3 ....

....

4 ....

....

5 ....

....

READING

3 Tessa has an unusual job. Look at the pictures and complete the text.

'I work on a bird sanctuary. I leave home at six thirty in the morning and
1 ....._cycle_..... three miles to the village. There I catch the seven o'clock
2 .... to Slimbridge. It's about ten miles away and
3 .... about half an hour. After that I 4 .... It's only
a mile from the bus stop to the 5 .... Then I get to the island in
a small 6 .... and arrive there at about quarter past eight.'

4 Write questions about Tessa's journey to work. Begin your questions with *How, How far* or *How long.*

YOU: ..._How do you get_.............. from your home to the village?

TESSA: I cycle.

YOU: ....

TESSA: It's about three miles.

YOU: .... from the village to Slimbridge?

TESSA: I go by bus.

YOU: ....

TESSA: About half an hour.

YOU: .... from Slimbridge to the island?

TESSA: I walk and then I go by boat.

YOU: ....

TESSA: Altogether? An hour and three quarters.

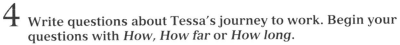

Unit 14

GRAMMAR: *there is/there are*

1 Ask questions and give short answers about the student's room in the picture.

1 carpet/floor

Is there a carpet on the floor?
Yes, there is.

2 pictures/walls

....

....

3 bag/wardrobe

....

....

4 books/desk

....

....

5 lamp/desk

....

....

READING

2 Read Jenny's letter about her college room and write short answers to the questions below.

> Student Hostel,
> Carnegie Hall,
> Wetherby Road,
> Leeds, LW 8??
> Yorks
>
> Monday
>
> Dear Ruth,
>
> I don't like the college hostel very much. It isn't very near the college and it isn't very modern.
>
> My room isn't very big. There isn't an armchair and there aren't any pictures on the walls. There's a bed, a wardrobe, a table and a chair but there isn't a bookcase for my books.
>
> I like the college, the students and the work!
>
> See you in December.
>
> Love,
> Jenny

1 Does Jenny like the college?
   Yes, she does.

2 Does Jenny like the hostel?
   ....

3 Is Jenny's hostel near the college?
   ....

4 Is Jenny's room small?
   ....

5 Is there an armchair in her room?
   ....

6 Are there any pictures on the walls?
   ....

WRITING

3 Imagine Jenny likes the hostel and her room. Rewrite the letter in your notebook. Change negative verbs to positive and change *but/or* to *and*. Begin like this:

Dear Ruth,
I like the college hostel very much. It ....

Unit 15

What are you doing, Daddy?

I'm ......*making*...... dinner. **1**

What are you doing now, Daddy?

I'm .... the recipe. **2**

What are you doing now, Daddy?

3

GRAMMAR: present continuous

1 Complete the bubbles using these verbs.

help	make	open
read	do	

2 Write the -ing form of the verbs in the correct columns.

open	go	do	have
make	read	write	listen
get	run	swim	ski
drive	use	walk	play
cycle	close	start	stop
end	finish	leave	arrive
watch	learn	clean	put

I'm .... a can. Ben, what are you .... ? **4**

I .... you, Daddy! **5**

+ ing	− e + ing	Double consonant + ing
opening	*making*	*getting*

26

WRITING

3
In your notebook, complete Mark's letter to a friend about his family. Write about his grandfather, mother, father, sister and brother and say what they are doing.

This is a photo of my family camping in France. My father is making dinner.

4 Complete the crossword.

CLUES

Across
1 You have this on the floor. (6)
4 You drink water and you ... breakfast. (3)
6 Helen is ... the newspaper in the sitting room. (7)
8 How do you ...? (2)
9 Elizabeth Morgan's initials. (2)
11 Not p.m. (2)
13 It's on top of the house. (4)
16 A preposition. (2)
17 You can see yourself in this. (6)

Down
2 Laura's address is 1, Hull ... (4)
3 What's the time? ... 's half past eight. (2)
5 A: What . . . is this building?
  B: It's about a hundred years old. (3)
7 Every room has one of these. (4)
10 ... name's Adam. (2)
11 ... there any chairs? (3)
12 He gets ... work at eight. (2)
14 We have ... lunch at twelve. When do you have your lunch? (3)
15 How ... is it to York? (3)

▄ *Listening and speechwork 11–15*

LISTENING

1 Listen to the dialogue and circle the correct answers.

1 Sue meets Harry
 a) in the street
 b) in his garden
 c) on a train

2 The time is
 a) 7 p.m.
 b) 7 a.m.
 c) 11 a.m.

3 Harry is
 a) jogging
 b) walking to the bus stop
 c) walking to work

4 The distance from his home to work is
 a) 9 miles
 b) 5 miles
 c) 15 miles

5 Harry usually
 a) goes by train
 b) walks
 c) goes by bus

6 He is walking today because
 a) he wants to keep fit
 b) his train is late
 c) there aren't any trains

2 Listen and look at the plans of two flats. Put a tick next to the correct flat.

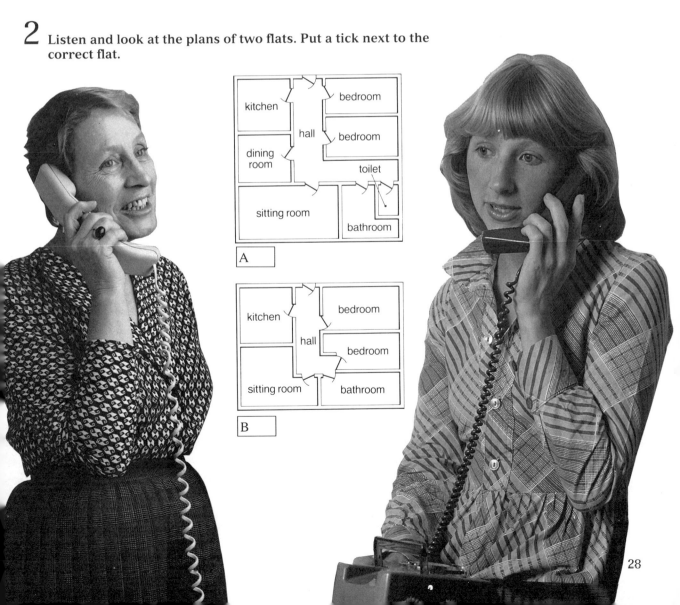

A

B

ORAL EXERCISES

3 Ask how often people drive to work.

(you/always)
s: *Do you always drive to work?*

1 you/always   4 they/sometimes
2 he/usually   5 you/never
3 she/often

4 Ask questions about time.

T: The concert starts at 6 o'clock.
(finish)
s: *What time does it finish?*

1 finish   3 end
2 close   4 arrive

5 Ask questions about what people are doing now.

T: John plays football every day.
s: *Is he playing football now?*

1 play football   4 write letters
2 play tennis   5 watch TV
3 clean the car   6 telephone her boyfriend

STRESS

6 Listen and underline the stressed words.

1 <u>What time</u> is it?
2 How far is it?
3 How long is it?
4 How old is it?
5 What are you doing?
6 Where are they going?

Now listen and repeat the questions.

PRONUNCIATION

Vowel sound
/ɜː/ He works in Germany.

7 Listen and repeat the words and phrases.

word   work   world
her   German   girl
learn   thirty German girls
His girlfriend works in Germany.
She's learning German at work.

Consonant sound
/h/ How are you?

8 Listen to the sentences and write the number of times you hear the sound /h/ in each sentence.

1 ...2...   4 ....

2 ....   5 ....

3 ....   6 ....

9 Listen and ask the questions.

T: I can see Harry.
s: *Who's Harry?*

1 Harry
2 Helen
3 Henry
4 Hilary

Unit 16

GRAMMAR: indefinite pronoun *one/ ones*

1 Write the answers. Choose the first item each time.

1 Do you want a black or a white T-shirt?

I'd like a black one, please.

2 Would you like the green or the red apples?

....

3 A large or a small coffee?

....

4 Would like a Japanese or a Swiss watch?

....

5 Which would you like, the Swiss or the Belgian chocolates?

....

COMMUNICATION

2 Complete the dialogue to buy the food and drink on the table.

A: .....*I'd*..... like a bottle of lemonade and a cup of ...*coffee*..., please.

B: Large or small?

A: ...., please.

B: Anything else?

A: Yes. ....
   a packet of crisps?

B: 20p.

A: O.K. .... have one, please?

B: Yes, certainly.

3 Rearrange these sentences to make a dialogue.

a It's £150.
b Can I help you?
c No, thanks. It's too expensive.
d Which one?
e Oh, that's very expensive.
f The very small automatic one.
g Yes, please. How much is that camera in the window?
h Do you want to look at it?

A: *Can I help you?* ....

B: ....

A: ....

B: ....

A: ....

B: ....

A: ....

B: ....

Unit 17

GRAMMAR: *have got/some* and *any*

1 Look at the food then ask and answer questions about Mr and Mrs Gibson.

1 *Have they got any* .... bananas?
  Yes, *they have.*

2 .... oranges?
  No, ...

3 .... eggs?
  ....

4 .... bread?
  ....

5 .... coffee?
  ....

2 Say what the Gibsons have and haven't got.

1 bananas/oranges
  They've got some bananas but they haven't got any oranges.

2 eggs/cheese
  ....
  ....

3 lager/wine
  ....
  ....

4 salt/sugar
  ....
  ....

5 biscuits/bread
  ....
  ....

6 tea/coffee
  ....
  ....

VOCABULARY: food and drink

3 Complete the crossword with words from Unit 17.

CLUES

Across
1 Unit 17 is about food and ... (5)
5 Potatoes and onions are ... (10)
8 ... and biscuits. (6)
9 ... and vinegar. (3)
10 ... and butter. (5)

Down
2 You cook food in a ... (7)
3 ... and sugar. (4)
4 . . . and chips. (4)
6 Salt and ... (6)
7 ... or coffee? (3)
8 Fish and ... (5)

Unit 18

THE MINSTER HOTEL
6, Davygate,
York YO5 2QE

Tel: 0904 653655

Our hotel is in the centre of the city. It is only 50 metres from York Minster and very near the theatre, shopping centre, cinemas and restaurants. There are 50 bedrooms, each with a bathroom, a colour TV and telephone. There is a car park behind the hotel.

READING

1 Read about the hotel and answer the questions.

1 What's the hotel called?
The Minster Hotel.

2 Where is it?
....

3 How far is it from York Minster?
....

4 How many bedrooms are there?
....

5 Have the bedrooms got colour TV?
....

6 Is there a car park?
....

7 Where is it?
....

8 Is there a swimming pool?
....

COMMUNICATION

2 Complete the dialogue with these phrases.

Where's the Minster Hotel?
Is there a car park near the hotel?
there's one
How far

A: Excuse me. *Where's the Minster Hotel?*

B: It's in Davygate in the city centre.

A: .... is that from here?

B: It's about half a mile.

A: ....

B: Yes, ... behind it.

VOCABULARY: prepositions of place

3 Look at the picture below and complete the sentences with the words in the box.

between	behind	in front of	on the left
under	next to	on the right	

1 Jenny is sitting ...*on the left*... of Natalie.

2 Emma is sitting .... of Natalie.

3 Paul is standing .... Richard.

4 Natalie is sitting .... Jenny and Emma.

5 Mr Robson is standing .... Jenny.

6 The dog is lying .... Natalie.

7 The cat is sitting .... the chair.

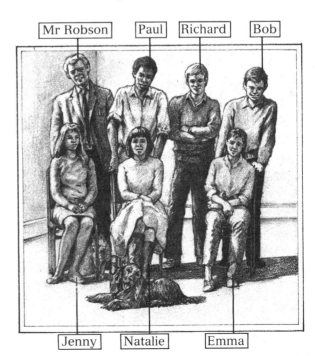

32

Unit 19

VOCABULARY: weather words

1 Write the word(s) for each sign.

1 It's *raining*

2 ....

3 ....

4 ....

5 ....

6 ....

7 ....

8 ....

READING

2 Read what a grandmother says to her grandson and answer the questions with the name of a month.

'When I was young, winters were very cold and summers were very hot. Autumn in September and October was beautiful but it was always foggy in November and it always snowed in December. It was windy in March, it rained in April, and it was always sunny in August. Nowadays the weather is different. It's always changing. It sometimes snows in April, rains in August and is warm and sunny in January!'

1 When was it always foggy? *November*

2 When did it always snow? ....

3 When was it windy? ....

4 When did it rain? ....

5 When was it always sunny? ....

6 When does it sometimes snow nowadays? ....

WRITING

3 Complete the text about the climate in your country.

The climate in .... is .... In

winter it .... and the temperature is about

.... In spring it .... and

.... In summer the weather is usually

.... and the temperature is about

.... Autumn is usually a ....

season in my country but sometimes ....

Unit 20

GRAMMAR: past simple

1 **Marcel lives in Calais in France. He spent a day in London. Write the verbs in the correct tense to tell the story.**

Last Monday Marcel (go) [1] ...*went*... to London

for the day. He (get up) [2]........................... at

6.30 a.m., travelled to Calais and then (go)

[3]................. to Dover by hovercraft. The

hovercraft (be) [4]................. late and he (not/

arrive) [5]........................... in Dover until 9 a.m.

He (go) [6]................. by train to London and

(arrive) [7]........................... at 11.15 a.m. Then he

(walk) [8]........................... to the museums but they

(not/be) [9]........................... open because it was

Monday.

He (have) [10]................. lunch in a restaurant but

the food (not/be) [11]................................... very

good. After lunch it (start) [12]...............................

to rain. He (go) [13]........................... to the Tower

of London but there (be) [14]................. lots of

tourists there and he (not/see) [15]...........................

.... very much. Then he (have) [16]................

a cup of coffee and at 4 o'clock he

(go) [17]................. shopping. Everything

(be) [18]................. very expensive.

He (get) [19]................. home at half past ten in the

evening. Marcel (not/enjoy) [20]...............................

.... his visit to London!

2 **Write short answers.**

1 Was the hovercraft on time?
No, it wasn't. ....

2 Were the museums open?

....

3 Was the food good?

....

4 Did it rain?

....

5 Were the shops expensive?

....

6 Did Marcel enjoy his visit?

....

3 **Write questions about Karen's trip to Budapest in Hungary.**

Trip to Hungary, Friday October 12th

6.30	get up
8.00	go to airport
8.30	check in
10.00	plane leaves London
13.35	plane arrives in Budapest
14.30	have lunch
16.00	go to museum

1 *What time did she get up?* ....
At 6.30 a.m.

2 ....
At 8.00 a.m.

3 ....
At 8.30 a.m.

4 ....
At 10.00 a.m.

5 ....
At 1.35 p.m.

6 ....
At 2.30 p.m.

7 ....
At 4.00 p.m.

WRITING

4 **Write a paragraph about Karen's trip to Budapest in your notebook. Begin like this:**

Karen got up at 6.30 a.m. and ....

LISTENING

1 Listen and correct the statements below.

1 The weather is warm and dry.
No, it's cold and wet. ....

2 Sarah and Derek want to find a baker's.
....

3 They find one next to the newsagent's.
....

4 They have tea and biscuits.
....

5 Sarah went to Italy for her holiday.
....

6 She went sightseeing every day.
....

2 Now listen again. Tick what Sarah and Derek order and fill in the prices.

```
——— MENU ———

Tea                          50p
Coffee          large  .........
                small   40p
Orange juice                 50p
Mineral water                60p
Sandwiches            .........
   Cheese and tomato
   Ham
   Egg
   Roast beef
   Hamburger           £1.50
```

ORAL EXERCISES

3 Ask for things in shops.

T: Can I help you?
s: *Yes, I'd like an evening newspaper, please.*

1 an evening newspaper
2 a box of matches
3 a tube of toothpaste
4 a litre of oil
5 two tickets for the seven o'clock performance

4 Ask how much things cost.

T: Yes, next please.
s: *How much is a ham sandwich?*
T: It's £1.25.

1 a ham sandwich
2 a packet of crisps
3 a portion of chips
4 a large cup of coffee
5 a small glass of orange juice

5 Ask people to get things for you.

T: Do you want anything at the shops?
s: *Yes, can you get me some tomatoes, please?*

1 tomatoes
2 newspaper
3 potatoes
4 battery
5 cigarettes

6 Say what the weather is like.

T: What's the weather like in January?
s: *It's usually cold.*
T: What's the weather like in February?
s: *It usually snows.*

1 January/cold
2 February/snows
3 March/cold and windy
4 April/rains
5 July/quite hot

1
2
3
4
5
6

7 Use the pictures to say where places are.

T: Is there a bank near here?
S: *Yes, there's one opposite the post office.*

1 bank
2 supermarket
3 hairdresser's
4 flower shop
5 video shop
6 car park

STRESS

8 Listen to the patterns.

1 <u>lots</u> of <u>milk</u>
2 <u>lots</u> of <u>butter</u>

Listen and say which pattern (1 or 2) these phrases follow.

1 fog in June ....1....

2 buy some pepper ....

3 rain in August ....

4 went to Spain ....

5 get some bread ....

6 stayed in London ....

Now listen and repeat the phrases.

PRONUNCIATION

> **Vowel sounds**
>
> /ɒ/ It's very | hot. |
>
> /əʊ/ I'm | go |ing | home. |

9 Listen and tick the sound you hear.

	/ɒ/	/əʊ/
1	✓	....
2	....	....
3	....	....
4	....	....
5	....	....
6	....	....

10 Listen and repeat the words and phrases.

Oh no   lots of snow   It snowed in October.
Oh no, not Joe.   Tom knows Joe.

> **Consonant sounds**
>
> /r/ That's | wrong. |
>
> /l/ That' | long. |

11 Listen and circle the word you hear.

1 (red)   lead
2 right   light
3 wrong   long
4 road   load
5 row   low
6 rate   late

12 Listen and repeat the phrases.

I like Laura.   The lights are red.
A letter for Laura.   Richard likes Laura.
A red one, please.

Unit 21

1 Write questions and answers to say who the items belong to.

1 Mr and Mrs Birch

2 Laura

3 Mrs Gibson

4 Adam

5 Michael

6 Mr and Mrs Gibson

1 *Whose is the car?*
  It's Mr and Mrs Birch's.

2 *Whose are the compact discs?*
  They're Laura's.

3 ....
  ....

4 ....
  ....

5 ....
  ....

6 ....
  ....

GRAMMAR: possessive pronouns

2 Rewrite the sentences using a possessive pronoun.

1 The car belongs to them.
  The car is theirs.

2 The cats belong to them.
  The cats are theirs.

3 The atlas belongs to me.
  ....

4 The compact discs belong to her.
  ....

5 The razor belongs to him.
  ....

6 The dogs belong to us.
  ....

7 The piano belongs to you.
  ....

8 The TV set belongs to them.
  ....

WRITING

3 Match the two parts of the sentences to describe the lost items.

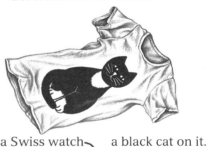

1 a Swiss watch   a black cat on it.
2 a T-shirt   some car keys in it.
3 a sports bag   gold letters on it.
4 an address book   a gold strap.
5 a handbag   some tennis balls in it.

1 *It's a Swiss watch with a gold strap.*
2 ....
3 ....
4 ....
5 ....

Unit 22

VOCABULARY: clothes

1 Write the words in the box in the correct groups. (Some clothes can go in more than one group.)

anorak	blouse	dress	shoes
cardigan	coat	jacket	tights
vest	stockings	jeans	shirt
shorts	socks	skirt	suit
trainers	trousers	boots	sweater

Clothes you wear on your top half.

1 *anorak*   5 ....

2 ....   6 ....

3 ....   7 ....

4 ....

Clothes you wear on your bottom half.

1 *tights*   4 ....

2 ....   5 ....

3 ....   6 ....

Clothes you wear on your top and bottom half.

1 *dress*

2 ....

3 ....

What you wear on your feet.

1 *shoes*

2 ....

3 ....

4 ....

WRITING

2 Write descriptions of the clothes the people are wearing.

Jason   Alison

1 Jason *is wearing a flowery shirt, jeans and trainers.*

2 Alison ....

....

George   Jeff and Lisa

3 George ....

....

4 Jeff and Lisa ....

....

Unit 23

Island in the sun
Special Summer Offer!
Two weeks for the price of one!
First 2 weeks of July only.

Half pension in the Hotel Napoleon in
Marina di Campo – only 2 minutes from the sea.

Fly from Manchester to Pisa, then by coach and boat.

SUMMER SAVERS Ltd, *Red Lion Square,*
Manchester MA4 BD6 tel: 061 345-8923

GRAMMAR: *going to* future

1 Look at the advertisement and write questions to complete the conversation.

YOU: When/have/holiday? [1] *When are you going to have your holiday?*

MIKE: In the first two weeks of July.

YOU: Where/go? [2] ....

....

MIKE: To Elba.

YOU: Elba! How lovely! How/get there?
[3] ....

MIKE: First by plane to Pisa and then by coach and boat.

YOU: That's quite a long journey. Where/stay?
[4] ....

MIKE: In a hotel in Marina di Campo.

YOU: That sounds nice. How long/stay?
[5] ....

MIKE: Two weeks.

YOU: Who/go with? [6] ....

....

MIKE: A group of three friends from the office.

YOU: Well, have a nice time!

COMMUNICATION: making suggestions

2 Use the chart to write conversations.

1 get	a Superman video	a James Dean video
2 have	a Chinese meal	fish and chips
3 give	a book about York Minster	a book about the Brontës

1 IN A VIDEO SHOP

A: What *are we going to get?*

B: What about *getting a Superman video?*

A: No, not *a Superman video* Let's *get a James Dean video* instead.

B: O.K. That's a good idea.

2 IN THE STREET AT 7.30 P.M.

A: What .... to eat?

B: ....

A: ....

....

B: ....

3 IN A BOOK SHOP

A: What .... Laura for her birthday?

B: .... her a

....

A: ....

....

B: ....

Unit *24*

VOCABULARY: adjectives of description

1 Circle the odd word in each group.

1 pretty   handsome   (ugly)   good-looking

2 nice   kind   interesting   beard

3 big   brown   blue   green

4 blonde   dark   fair   curly

5 beard   slim   glasses   moustache

COMMUNICATION: describing people

2 Ask about the person in the photograph. Complete the conversation using the correct questions from the box.

> Is she slim?
> Is it long?
> What colour are her eyes?
> What's she like?
> Is she tall?
> What colour hair has she got?

A: ¹ *What's she like?* ....

B: She's lovely. She's very friendly.

A: ² ....

B: No, she isn't. She's quite short.

A: ³ ....

B: They're brown.

A: ⁴ ....

B: It's dark.

A: ⁵ ....

B: Not really. It's medium length.

A: ⁶ ....

B: Yes, quite.

READING

3 Read the note and complete the information about Tony.

MESSAGES

My cousin, Tony, is arriving at the station on Monday. Can you meet him? He's small and slim and he's got grey, wavy hair, a small moustache and glasses.
Thanks,
Linda

Name	Height/Size	Hair: length/colour/style	Other features
Tony	small, ...	grey, ...	....
Sally	quite short	long, brown	glasses
Ted	big, tall	short, dark	a thin moustache
Andrew	tall	curly, red	a beard

WRITING

4 Use the chart in Exercise 3 to write similar notes about Sally, Ted and Andrew.

My friend, Sally, ...

....

....

....

My uncle, Ted, ...

....

....

....

My cousin, Andrew, ...

....

....

....

Unit 25

GRAMMAR: past simple

1 Look at the pictures and write questions and answers about what people did last weekend.

1 Sally/go to cinema

Did Sally go to the cinema?
No, she didn't. She went to the theatre

2 Robert/buy CD album

....

....

3 You and your friends/play tennis

....

....

4 You/wear a suit

....

....

5 Mr and Mrs Abbott/watch a quiz show

....

....

2 Complete the story with the past tense of the verbs in brackets.

Last year my wife and I (go) ¹....*went*........ to a friend's wedding in Italy. We (drive) ²........................ to Sorrento and then, after the wedding, we (do) ³........................ some sightseeing and (take) ⁴........................ some photographs. It (be) ⁵........................ quite hot and we (decide) ⁶........................ to go to a beach outside the city. We (change) ⁷........................ into our swimsuits and (leave) ⁸........................ our clothes, passports and cameras in the car in the car park. We (spend) ⁹........................ the day on the beach.

When we (get) ¹⁰........................ back to the car park at four o'clock, we (can) ¹¹........................ not find the car. We (have) ¹²........................ nothing except our swimsuits and a little money. We (buy) ¹³........................ some cheap clothes to wear and (tell) ¹⁴........................ the police. They (find) ¹⁵........................ the car two days later quite near the beach. Our passports, clothes and even our cameras (be) ¹⁶........................ in the car – and a note which (say) ¹⁷........................! 'Thanks for the ride! We (like) ¹⁸........................ the car very much. Ciao!'

WRITING

3 Link the three events to make two sentences using *and then* and *after that*.

	Event 1	Event 2	Event 3
1	have my evening meal	have a shower	go to the cinema
2	finish breakfast	read the paper	go back to bed
3	write some notes	make a plan	write the essay
4	go the bank	meet some friends	go home to lunch

1 *I had my evening meal and then I had a shower. After that I went to the cinema.*

2 ....

....

3 ....

....

4 ....

....

READING

4 Read the story and answer the questions.

THE £10 CAR

1 What was the advertisement for?
A Jaguar car. ....

2 How much did it cost?
....

3 What did Charlie do?
....

4 What did the car look like?
....

5 Whose car was it?
....

6 What did the woman's husband do last month?
....

7 Why did he write to her?
....

8 What did he ask his wife to do?
....

Last week my friend Charlie Baxter bought a magazine called 'Car Weekly'. He saw this advertisement in it: 'Jaguar XJS, two years old, one owner, £10'. Charlie telephoned immediately. A woman answered the phone. 'Are you sure the car is £10?' said Charlie.

'Sure,' said the woman

Five minutes later Charlie was in the woman's garage. There, in front of him, was the car. It was beautiful – large, shiny and silver. 'Are you sure the car is all right?' he asked.

'Yes,' said the woman. 'It's perfect.'

'Then why do you want to sell it?'

'My husband left me last month and went to live with another woman. Then he wrote and said he needed money. He said he didn't want to take any money from me so he asked me to sell his Jaguar and send him the money.' The woman smiled and said: 'And that's exactly what I'm doing.'

Listening and speechwork 21–25

LISTENING

1 Martin and Bob are at a conference. Bob wants to know who people are. Listen to the conversation and complete the information.

Name	Clothes	Height/Size	Hair
Sally	*red dress*		
Angus			
Sandra			

ORAL EXERCISES

2 Identify belongings.

T: Which is your jacket?
S: *That's mine.*

1 your jacket
2 Adam's desk
3 Laura's room
4 the Gibsons' house
5 our classroom

3 Say what people look like.

T: What's Simon like?
S: *He's tall and he's got blond hair.*

1 Simon/tall/blond hair
2 Tessa/medium height/short brown hair
3 Tony/quite short/red hair and a beard
4 your father/quite tall/grey hair and glasses
5 your sister/quite small/short curly hair

4 Talk about future plans.

T: What are your plans for next year?
S: *I'm going to work in Germany.*

1 work in Germany
2 work in a restaurant in Hamburg
3 live in a hostel
4 leave in October
5 start learning German next week

5 Ask about past events.

T: Ask Adam if he had a good weekend.
S: *Did you have a good weekend, Adam?*

1 Ask Adam if he had a good weekend.
2 Ask Laura if she went to the library this morning.
3 Ask Chris if she enjoyed her holiday in Barbados.
4 Ask her how long she spent there.
5 Ask Michael if he saw his girlfriend last night.

44

STRESS

6 Listen to the two patterns.

1 a <u>blue</u> <u>jacket</u>   2 an <u>orange</u> <u>tie</u>

Listen and write which pattern (1 or 2) these phrases follow.

1 a red sweater   ....
2 a yellow shirt   ....
3 an orange hat   ....
4 a green jacket   ....
5 a purple tie   ....
6 a blue blazer   ....

Now listen and repeat the phrases.

PRONUNCIATION

7 Listen and say if the sounds you hear are the same or different.

	Same	Different
1	....	✓ ....
2	....	....
3	....	....
4	....	....
5	....	....
6	....	....

8 Listen and repeat the words and phrases.

a sunny month   Can you come to lunch?
Sally can but her mum can't.
Sam has the money.

9 Listen and tick the sound you hear.

	/tʃ/	/ʃ/
1	...✓...	....
2	....	....
3	....	....
4	....	....
5	....	....
6	....	....

10 Listen and repeat the shopping list.

a Chinese shirt
a pair of cheap summer shoes
a chicken
a cheese sandwich
a bar of chocolate
sugar

Unit 26

COMMUNICATION: making arrangements

1 Look at Laura's diary and write the invitations and the answers.

1 go to/cinema/Monday or Tuesday evening

JOHN: *Would you like to go to the cinema on Monday evening?*

LAURA: *I'm sorry, I can't. I'm going to the theatre*

JOHN: *What about Tuesday?*

LAURA: *Yes, I'd love to.*

2 play tennis/Tuesday or Wednesday afternoon

SARAH: ....

LAURA: ....

SARAH: ....

LAURA: ....

3 have dinner/Thursday or Friday evening

ROGER: ....

LAURA: ....

ROGER: ....

LAURA: ....

4 spend the day with us/Saturday or Sunday

JAN: ....

LAURA: ....

JAN: ....

LAURA: ....

June

Monday 27 theatre 7.30 p.m.

Tuesday 28 3 p.m. go to dentist

Wednesday 29 have dinner with Janet 8 p.m.

Thursday 30 7.30 p.m. babysitting at the Henleys'

July

Friday 1 1 o'clock lunch with Mary

Saturday 2 go to Stratford for day

Sunday 3 free

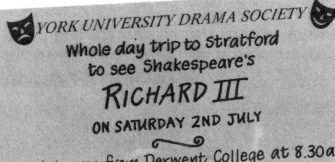

YORK UNIVERSITY DRAMA SOCIETY

Whole day trip to Stratford
to see Shakespeare's

RICHARD III

ON SATURDAY 2ND JULY

Coach leaves from Derwent College at 8.30 a.m.
and returns to college at approx. 9.30 p.m.

COST ONLY £15 (includes theatre ticket, coach fare, and a picnic lunch)

FRIENDS WELCOME

PLEASE BOOK YOUR PLACE BEFORE JUNE 25th

2 Read the notice and invite a friend to join you on the trip to Stratford. In your notebook, write a letter about your arrangements.

– say what the trip is about and what date it is
– invite your friend to join you
– say how much it costs
– say what time the coach leaves in the morning and returns in the evening.

Unit 27

Momo

TO: Robert Kerr

FROM: Your wife

MESSAGE:

Please call her back before 10 a.m.

NUMBER: The car phone number

COMMUNICATION: telephoning

1 Read the message and complete the telephone conversation with the words and phrases in the box.

> Can you   Thanks.   speak to   Who's speaking?
> call me back   I'm afraid   his wife
> the car phone

MAN: Good morning. Mr Kerr's telephone.

MRS KERR: Can I [1] ...***speak to***......... Robert, please?

MAN: [2] .... he's out at the moment.

MRS KERR: [3] .... take a message?

MAN: Certainly. [4] ....?

MRS KERR: It's [5] .... here.

MAN: Yes, Mrs Kerr.

MRS KERR: Can you ask him to [6] ....
             before ten o'clock. Tell him to use
             [7] .... number.
             I'm driving to his mother's house.

MAN: O.K. I'll tell him.

MRS KERR: [8] .... Goodbye.

2 Use the cues to write a telephone conversation.

LISA: Hello. Lisa speaking.

1 *Say who you are and ask to speak to Julie.*

YOU: ***Hello, it's (Maria) here. Can I speak to Julie, please?***

LISA: I'm sorry. She's not in at the moment.

2 *Ask if you can leave a message.*

YOU: ....

LISA: Yes, of course.

3 *Say you'd like Julie to meet you after work tomorrow.*

YOU: ....

....

LISA: After work tomorrow. Fine I'll tell her.

4 *Say thank you and goodbye.*

YOU: ....

LISA: Bye!

WRITING

3 Rearrange the parts of the sentences and write a message for an answerphone.

> 574 9985. Thanks. Bye!

> Hello. This is a message for

> call me back? My number is

> you both to lunch on

> here. I'd like to invite

> Ann and Julian. It's Sandy

> Sunday 23rd June. Can you

Hello, this is a message for

....

....

....

....

....

....

Unit 28

GRAMMAR: comparison of shorter adjectives

1 Write comparative and superlative adjectives in the spaces on the chart.

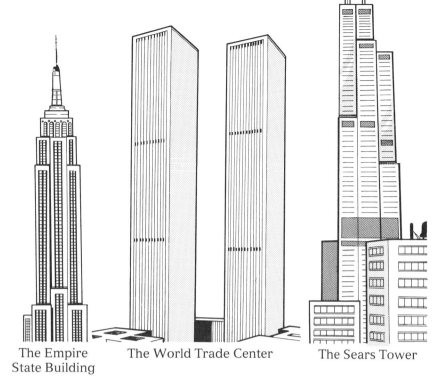

The Empire State Building   The World Trade Center   The Sears Tower

1 TALL

The Empire State Building, New York 1,250 ft 381 m	The World Trade Center, New York 1,350 ft 411 m	The Sears Tower, Chicago 1,454 ft 443 m
tall	*taller*	*tallest*

2 LONG

The Mississippi 3,710 miles 5,970 km	The Nile 4,053 miles 6,522 km	The Yangtze 3,340 miles 5,375 km
		long

3 BIG

China 3,745,000 sq miles 9,699,550 sq km	Canada 3,851,809 sq miles 9,976,186 sq km	The USSR 8,650,000 sq miles 22,403,500 sq km

4 COLD

Copenhagen −3°C	Moscow −10°C	Berlin −1°C

5 HOT

Cairo 32°C	Istanbul 30°C	Athens 29°C

2 Write sentences.

1 *The World Trade Center is taller than the Empire State Building but the Sears Tower is the tallest.*

2 ....

3 ....

4 ....

5 ....

VOCABULARY

3 Write the opposites. Choose from the adjectives in the box.

old cold bad early dirty small wet long short fat low

bigger ..... *smaller* .....

cleaner ....

drier ....

later ....

better ....

higher ....

hotter ....

shorter ....

taller ....

thinner ....

younger ....

READING

4 Read the text about Indonesia and answer the questions.

1 How many islands does Indonesia consist of?

....

2 How long is its coastline?

....

3 How long (approximately) is Canada's coastline?

....

4 How many nations are larger than Indonesia?

....

Coastline of islands

INDONESIA

INDONESIA is in South East Asia. It consists entirely of islands. There are about 3,000 of them. It has the world's second longest coastline at 54,680 km (33,978 miles) but it is only the fifteenth largest nation. The nation with the longest coastline is Canada, which is five times larger than Indonesia.

Unit 29

GRAMMAR: comparison of longer adjectives

Buy a present from the hospital shop and make someone happy!

Bunch of flowers	£3.25
Bunch of grapes	£2.75
Packet of biscuits	55p
Box of chocolates	£5.95
Music cassette	£4.99
Story cassette	£3.99
Paperback book	£2.95
Magazine	£1.50

1 Compare the prices of the items in the shop.

1 box of chocolates/bunch of flowers

A box of chocolates is more expensive than a bunch of flowers.

2 bunch of flowers/bunch of grapes

....

....

3 a packet of biscuits/box of chocolates

....

....

4 a music cassette/a story cassette

....

....

5 magazine/book

....

....

2 Complete the statements with the superlative form of one of the adjectives in the box.

interesting	difficult	beautiful	polluted
dangerous	fashionable		

1 Florence is one of the *most beautiful* cities in the world.

2 This is one of the .... books about Greek civilization.

3 New York is one of the ....
.... cities in the USA.

4 Paris and Milan are two of the ....
.... cities in Europe.

5 Chinese is probably one of the ....
.... languages to learn for British people.

6 The Thames is one of the ....
.... rivers in Britain.

WRITING

3 In your notebook, rewrite the paragraph correcting the mistakes.

PARIS

I think Paris is one of ^ most
beautiful (citys) in the world.   **Sp**
I think it is ^ best city for a
Sp (holliday). Perhaps the (french   **P**
are not so friendly but I think
Sp they are (friendlyer) (that) the   **G**
P (english! The (better) time to   **G**
visit Paris is in the spring.
G (I'm going) there every year
G but it is (more hard) now to
find a cheap hotel.

Unit 30

GRAMMAR: mixed tenses

1 Write the correct form of the verbs in brackets (present simple, present continuous or past simple).

Dear Penny,

I (arrive) ......*arrived*...... in England from Sweden last September. At the moment I (live) .... with a nice family and (work) .... as their au pair. Everyone asks me if I (enjoy) .... my stay in England. Well, the answer (be) .... yes and no. I like my family, but they (go out) .... a lot in the evenings and I (be) .... often alone. I (start) .... English classes last week and now my English (get) .... a little better. But my problem is that I (not know) .... many English people.

Can you help me?

Ulla, Manchester, England

Dear Penny

Penny Jones answers your letters

GETTING TO KNOW THE RUSSIANS

MARIAN MARTIN is from Inverness in Scotland. At the moment she is working at a hostel for university students in Aberdeen. She is planning to take a holiday in the USSR next year. 'I'm working hard to pay for my holiday.' Marian is learning Russian at home. 'I prefer working on my own because I'm a slow learner.'

THINKING EUROPEAN

MATHIEU FAURET is a Frenchman from Lyon. He's working in London at the moment. He is learning German because he is hoping to work in Austria next year. 'I want to learn German for business.' Mathieu is having classes at work with a private teacher. 'I learn faster with one teacher than in a class.'

WORKING ABROAD

SANDRA WIGGIN'S home is in Wales. She started a temporary job in September with a holiday company in York. She wants to work in Meribel, a ski resort in France. 'I want to speak French better and get a permanent job abroad. At the moment I am learning French at evening classes. It's hard work but I'm learning quite fast.'

READING

2 Read the texts on the left-hand page and complete the information in the chart.

	Marian	Mathieu	Sandra
Where are they from?	*Scotland*		
Where are they working?			
What language are they learning?			
Where are they studying?			

WRITING

3 Write about each of the three people. Write three sentences like this.

1 Marian *is from Scotland. At the moment she is working in Aberdeen. She wants to go to the USSR and is learning Russian at home*

2 Mathieu ....

....

....

3 Sandra ....

....

....

4 Now write about Julio in the same way.

Home town:	Mexico City
Job:	journalist
Temporary activity:	working for the American magazine *Newsweek* in New York
Travel plans:	Europe
Languages:	English and French at a private language school in New York.

Julio is a journalist from ....

....

....

....

Listening and speechwork 26–30

LISTENING

1 Listen and complete the information on the poster.

THE LONDON JAZZ FESTIVAL

at
The London Arena,
Docklands

on _____

Tickets at £_____, £_____
and £_____. Available from all
ticket agencies

Credit Card Hotline
01 _____

ORAL EXERCISES

2 Invite people to do things.

s: *Would you like to come to lunch?*
t: Yes, I'd love to.

1 come to lunch
2 sit next to the window
3 look at this magazine
4 see my holiday photographs
5 meet my family
6 see something of the city

3 Arrange dates.

t: What about meeting on January 4th?
s: *Well, January 5th is better for me.*

1 January 4th/5th
2 February 1st/2nd
3 August 2nd/3rd
4 September 15th/16th
5 May 29th/30th
6 June 30th/July 1st

4 Compare things.

t: I'm afraid the bill for your car is £120.
s: *Oh, it's more expensive than I thought.*

1 I'm afraid the bill for your car is £120.
2 This watch is only £4.99.
3 John Cleese is nearly 1m 95cm tall.
4 Their house is over a hundred years old.
5 The temperature is already 35°C!
6 Kylie Minogue is only 1m 62cm tall.

5 Talk on the telephone.

MESSAGE

Can you please phone
Martin Page on 654755
and tell him that I'm
now arriving on
Monday 23rd, not
Sunday 22nd.

Thanks,
Sue (Winters)

Look at the note above. Telephone Martin Page to give him the message.

MAN: Hello. 654755. LMS Services. Can I help you?

YOU: ¹ *Can I speak to* Martin Page, please?

MAN: Yes, who's speaking, please?

YOU: ² ....

MAN: One moment . . . I'm sorry he's not here.

YOU: ³ .... a message?

MAN: Yes, of course. Hold on, I'll get a pen. Right, what is the message?

YOU: ⁴ ....

....

MAN: Sorry, can you say that again, please?

YOU: ⁵ ....

....

MAN: O.K. I'll give him the message.

YOU: ⁶ ....

MAN: You're welcome. Goodbye.

YOU: ⁷ ....

Now listen to someone giving the same message and check your answer.

STRESS

6 The weak form /ə/ has many spellings in English. Listen and circle the weak /ə/ syllables in these phrases and sentences.

1 Older than me.
2 Cheaper and better.
3 Britain and France
4 The police are here.
5 John's parents are at home.
6 An apple and a banana.

Now listen and repeat the phrases and sentences.

PRONUNCIATION

Vowel sounds
/e/ [Let]'s go.
/eɪ/ It's [late].

7 Listen and write how many times you hear the sound /eɪ/ in each sentence.

1 ...*1*....   4 ....
2 ....   5 ....
3 ....   6 ....

8 Listen and repeat the words and phrases.

Let's go to bed.
Henry is late.
They went to bed at eight.
She ate some bacon and eggs for breakfast.
Wednesday 8th May.

Consonant sounds
The linking /r/
bigg[er a]nd better

9 Listen and repeat the phrases. Try to link /r/ with *and* each time.

cheaper and better   mother and daughter
bigger and taller   sugar and milk
cleaner and nicer   more and more
father and mother

Unit 31

COMMUNICATION

1 Write the questions and answers for each of the pictures.

1 *Would you like something to drink?*
Yes, please. I think I'll have a lemonade.

2 *Would you like something to eat?*

....

3 ....

....

4 ....

....

5 ....

....

2 Complete the conversation in a café.

WAITRESS: Are you ready to order?

CUSTOMER: Yes. Can ......*I have*...... the chicken, please.

WAITRESS: And what vegetables .... like?

CUSTOMER: .... like some mushrooms, please.

WAITRESS: And what .... to drink?

CUSTOMER: I .... have some mineral water, please.

GRAMMAR: *I'd/I'll*

3 Complete the sentences with *I'd* or *I'll*.

1 I think ...*I'll*... have the fish, please.

2 .... like a glass of orange juice.

3 .... have milk with my coffee, please.

4 .... like a table near the window, please.

5 I think .... have the spaghetti bolognese, please.

6 .... ask for the bill.

VOCABULARY

4 Label the ingredients on the kitchen table.

4

1 *wine*

2

5

3

6

Unit 32

GRAMMAR: present perfect

1 Complete the table.

Present	Past	Past participle
Regular drop	*dropped*	*dropped*
pass	....	....
happen	....	....
look	....	....
Irregular break	*broke*	*broken*
win	....	....
find	....	....
lose	....	....
see	....	....
hurt	....	....

COMMUNICATION

2 Write the correct form of the verbs in brackets to complete the conversation.

MR GIBSON: What's wrong?

MRS GIBSON: I think I (lose) [1] *'ve lost* ....
my ring.

MR GIBSON: (you look) [2] ....
in the bedroom?

MRS GIBSON: Yes, I have.

MR GIBSON: What about the kitchen?

MRS GIBSON: I (look) [3] .... in
the kitchen. It isn't there.

Wait a moment. I (not look) [4] ....:

.... in the bathroom.

Yes, here it is!

MR GIBSON: Oh good.

MRS GIBSON: Oh no! I (just drop) [5] ....

.... it down the washbasin!

GRAMMAR: tense revision

3 Write the verb in brackets in the correct form.

1 Don't (drop) .... *drop* .... that Chinese vase. It's very old.

2 Julie is very happy. She's just (pass) ....
her exam.

3 In this competition you can (win) .... a car.

4 She fell off her horse and (break) ....
her arm.

5 Ladies and gentlemen, we are now (arrive)

.... at Charles de Gaulle airport.
Please fasten your seatbelts.

6 I've just (receive) .... a long letter from
my niece in Zimbabwe.

VOCABULARY

4 Circle the word in the group that cannot follow the verb.

1 *break* cup (carpet) glass leg

2 *win* competition car water money

3 *drop* book glass house cup

4 *lose* money glasses wallet factory

Unit 33

GRAMMAR: present perfect

1 Use the picture and the verbs in the box to ask questions.

| see   read   be   sleep   play   eat |

1   *Have you ever read 'The Russia House' by John le Carré?*

2   ....

3   ....

4   ....

5   ....
     ....

6   ....
     ....

3 paella

COMMUNICATION

2 Circle the correct answers in the conversation.

1 A: Have you ever a) gone to China?
                      b) been to China?
                      c) been in China?

2 B: Yes, I a) have.
              b) been.
              c) do.
   A: When did you go?

3 B: I a) have gone last year.
         b) did go last year.
         c) went last year.

4 A: a) Have you seen the Great Wall?
      b) Did you see the Great Wall?
      c) Were you seeing the Great Wall?
   B: Yes, it was fantastic.

5 A: You're lucky. a) I never seen it.
                     b) I never see it.
                     c) I've never seen it.

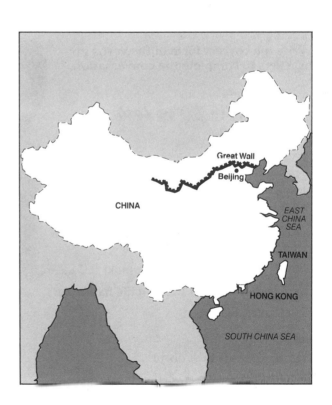

READING AND WRITING

3 Use the cards, the verbs in the box and
your own information to complete the
letter to a friend in your notebook.

come back   go   get   have

(Your address)

....

....

....

.... (date)

Dear ....,(friend's name)

Quite a lot has happened recently. Joe and Cindy

have just .... Jack Hayward

.... Sarah Jones ....

and Jeremy Saunders .... And what

about me? Well, I .... (your news)

Please write and tell me your news!

Love from

.... (Your name)

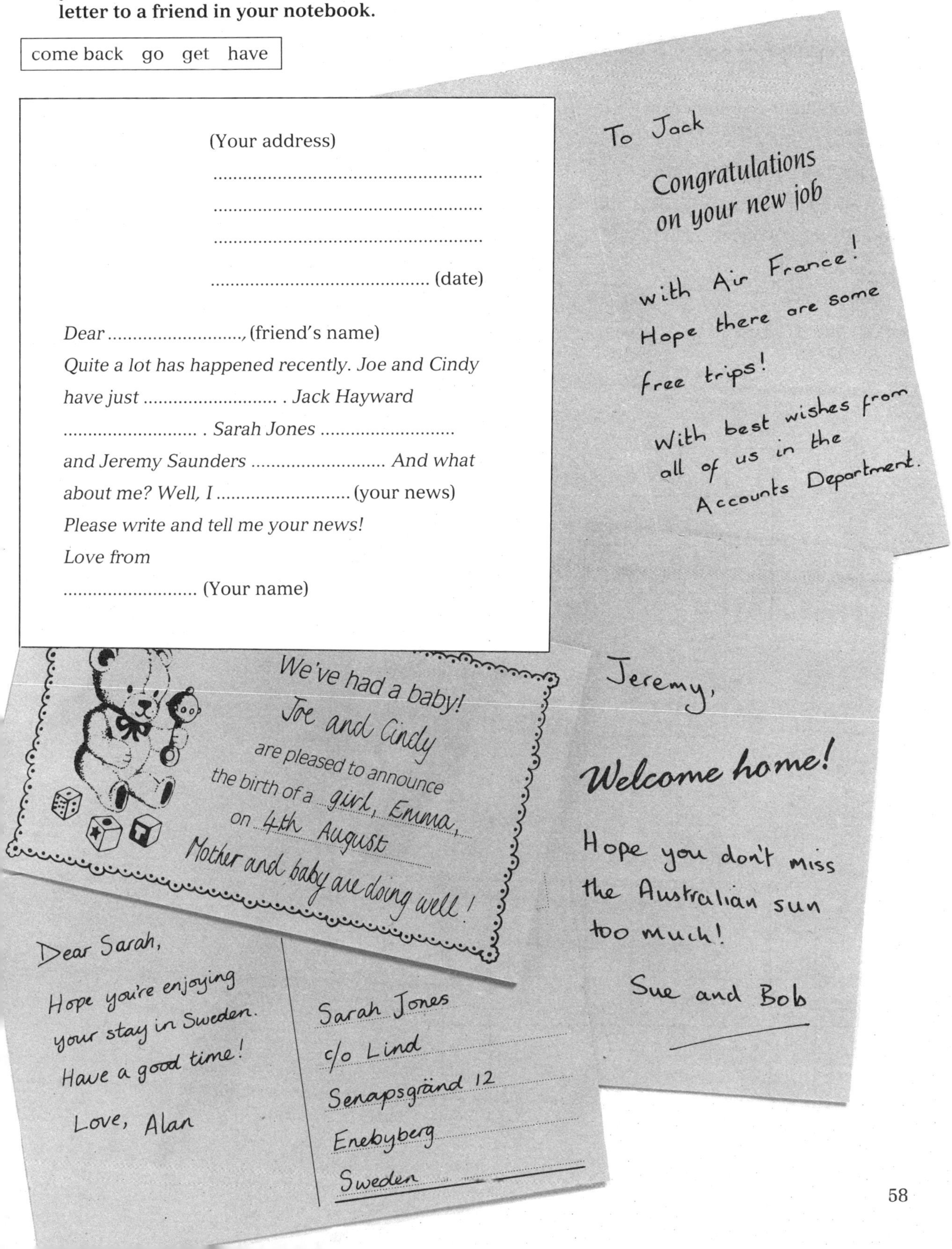

To Jack

Congratulations
on your new job

with Air France!
Hope there are some
free trips!

With best wishes from
all of us in the
Accounts Department.

We've had a baby!

Joe and Cindy
are pleased to announce
the birth of a girl, Emma,
on 4th August

Mother and baby are doing well!

Jeremy,

Welcome home!

Hope you don't miss
the Australian sun
too much!

Sue and Bob

Dear Sarah,

Hope you're enjoying
your stay in Sweden.

Have a good time!

Love, Alan

Sarah Jones

c/o Lind

Senapsgränd 12

Enebyberg

Sweden

Unit 34

GRAMMAR: possessive adjectives

1 **Complete the sentences with the correct possessive adjectives.**

1 i think I've hurt ...*my*... arm.

2 I'm afraid he's broken .... ankle.

3 What's the matter with her? Has she hurt .... foot?

4 Look! You've cut .... finger!

5 Poor dog! It's hurt .... leg.

VOCABULARY: parts of the body

2 **Look at the photograph and complete the crossword with the parts of the body.**

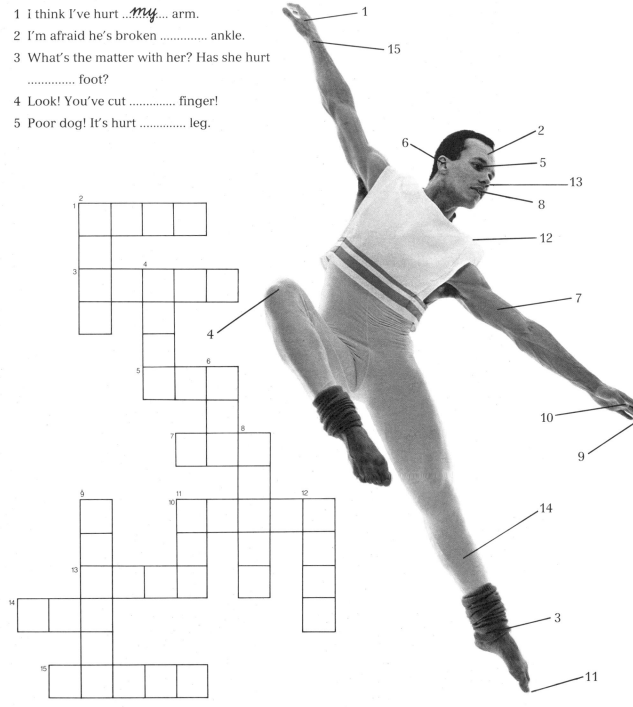

COMMUNICATION

3 Complete the conversation using the words in the box.

don't feel matter?
sore throat it is. what
Would you like speaking?
It's I've got Is that

LIZ: Hello. ¹ *Is that* Kevin?

KEVIN: Yes, ² .... Who's ³ ....

LIZ: ⁴ .... Liz here. ⁵ .... to come swimming this evening?

KEVIN: I'm afraid I can't. I ⁶ .... very well.

LIZ: Oh, what's the ⁷ ....

KEVIN: I've got a ⁸ .... and a headache. I think ⁹ .... a cold.

LIZ: Oh, ¹⁰ .... a nuisance! I hope you're better soon.

4 Write another dialogue.

John phones Richard. He asks Richard to play tennis with him tomorrow morning. Richard doesn't feel very well. He's got a temperature and he's in bed.

JOHN: ....

RICHARD: ....

JOHN: ....

....

RICHARD: ....

JOHN: ....

RICHARD: ....

JOHN: ....

READING

5 Rearrange the paragraphs to tell the story.

A A few days later, Mrs Smith came back and asked for another wooden leg. Again the doctor gave her a leg but this time he said: 'Please tell your husband to be careful. Wooden legs are very expensive.'

B 'Nothing's the matter with me. It's my husband. I'm afraid he's broken his wooden leg. Could you give him a new one, please?' 'Certainly,' said the doctor and signed the form.

C Mrs Smith looked at the doctor and said: 'To tell you the truth, doctor, he's making a coffee table.'

D 'Good afternoon, Mrs Smith,' said the doctor. 'What's the matter with you?'.

E But Mrs Smith was back the next day and the next. By now the doctor was very suspicious and said to Mrs Smith: 'What on earth is your husband doing with all these wooden legs? I've now given you four!'

Correct order:

1 *D*   2 .....   3 .....   4 .....   5 .....

Unit 35

COMMUNICATION

1 Look at Neil's list of things to do and complete the conversation.

> hairdresser's 9.30 a.m.
> • dentist's 11.00 a.m.
> • meet my mother for lunch
> • see bank manager 2.30 p.m.
> • go to work 3 p.m.

1 JILL: I've got a day off tomorrow. Can we meet to go shopping at 9.45?

NEIL: *I'm afraid I've got to go to the hairdresser's at 9.30*

2 JILL: Well, let's have coffee after your hair appointment.

NEIL: ....

....

3 JILL: What about lunch then?

NEIL: ....

....

4 JILL: Oh, well. What about meeting in the afternoon?

NEIL: ....

....

5 JILL: O.K. One last try. Let's have tea together at 3.30.

NEIL: ....
But I'm free all day Wednesday!

GRAMMAR: *have got to*/infinitive of purpose

2 Match a place with a purpose to write sentences.

PLACE	PURPOSE
1 shops	book some tickets to Madrid
2 post office	get some milk and bread
3 passport office	collect a parcel
4 shoe shop	get a visa
5 travel agent's	return some shoes

1 I*'ve got to go to the shops to get some milk and bread.*

2 She ....

....

3 You ....

....

4 He ....

....

5 We ....

....

WRITING

3 Sort the different parts of the letter and then write it in your notebook.

A   sorry we're going to miss the party but

B   has got to go to Warsaw to do some business and I'm going with her. I'm

C   Dear Julia and Ted,
It was very nice to get your letter and to hear your news. Thank you

D   we can't change the dates of the trip. We'll

E   ring when we get back to hear about the party.
Love,
Mike

F   very much for the invitation to your wedding anniversary party. Unfortunately Paula

 Listening and speechwork 31–35

LISTENING

1 Listen to the conversation and circle the correct answer.

1 The man and woman are going to
   a) the theatre.
   (b) the cinema.
   c) a concert.

2 They're going to have something to eat in
   a) a restaurant.
   b) a pub.
   c) a café.

3 The woman says that
   a) she has eaten Spanish food before.
   b) she loves Spanish food.
   c) she has never been to a Spanish restaurant before.

4 The man orders
   a) a potato dish.
   b) a dish called 'tapas'.
   c) a tomato salad.

5 The woman wants to go home because
   a) she's got a stomachache and feels dizzy.
   b) she's got a very bad headache.
   c) she needs to get some cigarettes.

6 The man offers
   a) to get her some medicine.
   b) to buy her some cigarettes.
   c) to call a taxi.

ORAL EXERCISES

1 a cup of tea

2 an ice cream

3 a glass of wine

4 a sandwich

5 a piece of cake

6 a cup of coffee

2 Offer things to eat and drink.

s: *Would you like a cup of tea?*

3 Look at the pictures in Exercise 2 again and decide what to have.

T: Would you like something to drink?
s: *Yes, please. I think I'll have a cup of tea.*

4 Talk about experiences.

T: Have you ever been to Paris?
s: *No, I've never been to France.*

1 Paris (France)
2 Buenos Aires (Argentina)
3 Sydney (Australia)
4 Lisbon (Portugal)
5 Budapest (Hungary)
6 Kyoto (Japan)

5 Ask what the matter is.

T: Oh! My head!
s: *What's the matter? Have you got a headache?*

1 Oh! My head!
2 Atishoo! Atishoo!
3 Oh! My tooth.
4 Have you got any throat pastilles?
5 Cough! Cough!
6 I feel terribly hot.

6 Say where you've got to go.

T: I need to get some money for the weekend.
s: *Yes, I've got to go to the bank too.*

1 bank
2 post office
3 video shop
4 library
5 chemist's
6 newsagent's

STRESS

7 Listen to the stress pattern.

I've got to buy some bread

Now listen and underline the words which carry the main stress in these sentences.

1 I want to go to bed.

2 She's got to go to school.

3 He came to buy the fridge.

4 He's got to leave at nine.

5 She's got a nasty cold.

6 I'd like some bread and cheese.

7 I've bought a loaf of bread.

Now listen and repeat the sentences. Try to say them all with the same rhythm.

PRONUNCIATION

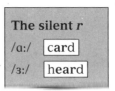

The silent *r*
/ɑː/ card
/ɜː/ heard

8 Sometimes you can hear *r* and sometimes you can't. Listen and circle the silent *r*.

1 train
2 hair
3 there
4 are
5 hearing
6 learning to read
7 four
8 mother and father

9 Listen and repeat the words and phrases.

are   part   card   car park
or   port   four
learn   work   heard
fair   hair   wear
near   here   dear
It's quite near here.
The car's in the car park.
He's working hard.

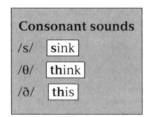

Consonant sounds
/s/ sink
/θ/ think
/ð/ this

10 Listen and repeat the phrases.

Sam thinks you're right.
I thought so.
This is very thick.
Thank you so much.
He's so thin.
That's the third time.
There's the bus.

Unit 36

COMMUNICATION

1 Complete the dialogue with the correct sentences.

Can I try this on?
I think I'll leave it.
It's too small. Have you got it
  in a larger size?
Have you got this in black?
Do you take credit cards?

> **1** *Have you got this in black?*
>
> There are some over there.

> **2**
>
> That's all we've got.

> **3**
>
> Sure. The changing rooms are over there.

> **4**
>
> No, I'm afraid we don't.

> **5**
>
> O.K.

GRAMMAR: *too* + adjective/ comparison of adjectives

2 Say what is wrong and ask a question.

New for Spring!

Silk blouses
now at
£65.00
Italian handbags
now only
£95.00

A customer wants to buy a short white jacket, a long black skirt, a white blouse, a small black hat and a handbag. She is a size 14 and has £100 to spend.

1 GIRL: The blouse is silk. It's only £65.

CUSTOMER: *I'm afraid it's too expensive. Have you got a cheaper one?*

2 GIRL: The long jacket is our latest style.

CUSTOMER: ....

....

3 GIRL: Don't you like the big hat?

CUSTOMER: ....

....

4 GIRL: The bag is only £95.

CUSTOMER: ....

....

5 GIRL: The short skirt is nice, isn't it?

CUSTOMER: ....

....

VOCABULARY

3 Complete the crossword.

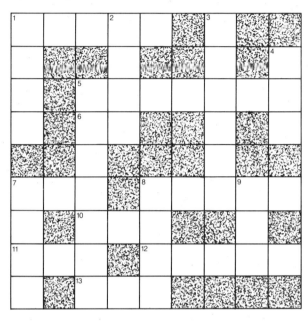

CLUES

Across

1 Nationality adjective from Switzerland
5 This is too large. Have you got a . . . size?
6 You and I
7 A drink
8 Do you take credit . . .?
10 I'm afraid this is . . . small.
11 A: Which jacket do you like?
   B: I like the green . . .
12 Not small
13 A colour

CLUES

Down

1 A: What . . . are you?
   B: I'm . . . 14.
2 Would you like . . . milk?
3 What . . . do you want? Black or red?
4 Can I . . . these shoes on, please?
5 You wear it when it's cold.
7 Past tense of *take*
8 Not hot
9 An animal

Unit 37

GRAMMAR: Adjectives and adverbs of manner

1 Write *ADJ* if the underlined words are adjectives and *ADV* if they are adverbs.

1 He's a <u>fast</u> driver.   *ADJ*

2 She waited <u>nervously</u> outside the door.   ....

3 He always works very <u>hard</u>.   ....

4 She's very <u>friendly</u>.   ....

5 She speaks very <u>good</u> English.   ....

6 He sings <u>beautifully</u>.   ....

7 He swims <u>well</u>.   ....

VOCABULARY: adverbs of manner

2 Write the opposite adverbs.

...*quickly*... slowly

.... noisily

.... badly

.... late

.... quickly

.... rudely

.... sadly

.... confidently

GRAMMAR: negative instructions

3 A father has a list of things he doesn't like about his teenage son. Rewrite each complaint as a request.

1 *Please don't play your music so loudly.*

2 ....
....

3 ....
....

4 ....
....

5 ....
....

6 ....
....

He plays his music too loudly.
He uses the telephone too often.
He eats his food very quickly.
He drives his motorbike too fast.
He speaks to his sister very rudely.
He slams the front door very noisily.

66

GRAMMAR: modal verbs *must*, *mustn't*, *can* and *can't*

1 Write a rule for the swimming pool for each diagram. Use *must* and *mustn't* and the verbs and expressions in the box.

> look after small children
> wear a swimming cap
> have a shower before you swim
> run   shout or scream
> eat or drink in the pool area

1 *You must wear a swimming cap*

2 ....

3 ....

4 ....

5 ....
   ....

6 ....

LIBRARY RULES
Branwell College Library
Hours: M-F 8 a.m.–6 p.m.   Sat 9 a.m.–12 p.m.

- Don't take more than three books at any one time.
- Return all books after one week.
- Do not take reference books out of the library.
- No talking, no eating, no drinking, no litter.

2 Complete the library rules with *can, must* or *can't*.

1 You ....*can*.... take out three books but you ....*can't*.. keep them longer than a week.

2 You .... take three books home but you .... return them after one week.

3 You .... read reference books in the library but you .... take them home.

4 You .... use the library on Saturday afternoon.

5 You .... take any food into the library.

3 Read the examination rules and tick what you can or can't do.

> EXAMINATIONS   June 1st–20th
>
> - Examinations start at 9 a.m. and finish at 12 noon.
> - Do not enter the examination room after 9.15 a.m.
> - Calculators and dictionaries are allowed.
> - Food, drinks and cigarettes are not allowed.
>
> Please note that students MUST pay all examination fees by May 1st.

Can you	Can	Can't
1 pay your exam fee on June 1st?	....	✓
2 arrive at 9.10 a.m.?	....	....
3 take a bar of chocolate with you?	....	....
4 use a dictionary?	....	....
5 take a drink with you?	....	....
6 use a calculator?		....

Unit 39

VOCABULARY: adjectives of feeling and emotion

1 Write the adjectives in the box in two columns: positive or negative.

> happy   sad   frightened   cheerful
> depressed   lonely   worried   pleased
> bored   excited   nervous   upset

Positive feelings	Negative feelings
happy	*sad*
....	....
....	....
....	....
	....
	....
	....
	....

2 Look at the faces and write a suitable adjective under each face.

1 *nervous*   2 ....

3 ....   4 ....   5 ....   6 ....

GRAMMAR: time clause *when* + present tense

3 Choose an adjective from the box and write sentences.

> happy   nervous   excited   homesick
> frightened   upset

1 wake up on a sunny day
   When I wake up on a sunny day, I feel happy

2 think about our trip to the USA
   ....
   ....

3 travel by plane
   ....
   ....

4 lose something valuable
   ....
   ....

5 am away from home for a long time
   ....
   ....

6 watch a horror film late at night
   ....
   ....

COMMUNICATION

4 Rearrange the answers to write an interview with Victoria Wood, a popular British TV and stage comedian.

INTERVIEWER: What is your idea of happiness?

VICTORIA: 1 *Four library books and some toast.*

INTERVIEWER: What objects do you always take with you?

VICTORIA: 2 ....

INTERVIEWER: What or who is the greatest love of your life?

VICTORIA: 3 ....

INTERVIEWER: What are you most frightened of?

VICTORIA: 4 ....

INTERVIEWER: What sort of things upset you most?

VICTORIA: 5 ....

INTERVIEWER: Which living person do you most hate?

VICTORIA: 6 ....

INTERVIEWER: When and where were you happiest?

VICTORIA: 7 ....

INTERVIEWER: How do you feel at the moment?

VICTORIA: 8 ....

Answers

 My husband, Geoff, and my daughter, Gracie.

I get upset when things go wrong in the house.

I feel quite pleased with life, actually.

My purse, three cheque books, my toothbrush and a banana.

At the Rochdale Youth Theatre Workshop, in the summer of 1968.

Four library books and some toast.

Hitting somebody in my car.

I don't hate anyone.

Unit 40

GRAMMAR: prepositions of time

1 Complete the sentences with *for, ago, in* or *on*.

1 He was born ...*in*.... 1967.

2 They got married two years ....

3 The Brontë Sisters lived .... the 19th century.

4 She lived in Paris .... several years.

5 He worked in Brazil .... about five years.

6 A few years .... she went to the USA.

7 She was born .... 17th July 1989.

8 He died ten years ....

9 They always have a family party .... Christmas Day.

10 We're going on holiday .... two weeks in December.

READING

2 Read the paragraph and answer the questions.

1 Where was Naomi James born?
   (She was born) in New Zealand.

2 When did she go to Britain?
   ....

3 What did she do first?
   ....

4 How long did she do that?
   ....

5 When did she learn to sail?
   ....

6 When did she sail around the world?
   ....

7 How old was she when she sailed around the world?
   ....

8 How long did her journey take?
   ....

9 Why is she famous?
   ....
   ....

Dame Naomi James, the first and fastest woman to sail alone around the world.

First and fastest

NAOMI JAMES was born in New Zealand in 1949. In 1970 she went to Britain and worked as a language teacher for five years. In 1975 she got a job with a yacht company and learned to sail. Two years later Naomi James was famous. She was the first woman to sail alone around the world. Her journey was also the fastest. It took just under 272 days.

WRITING

3
Correct the mistakes in this biography of the American composer, Cole Porter, and rewrite it in your notebook.

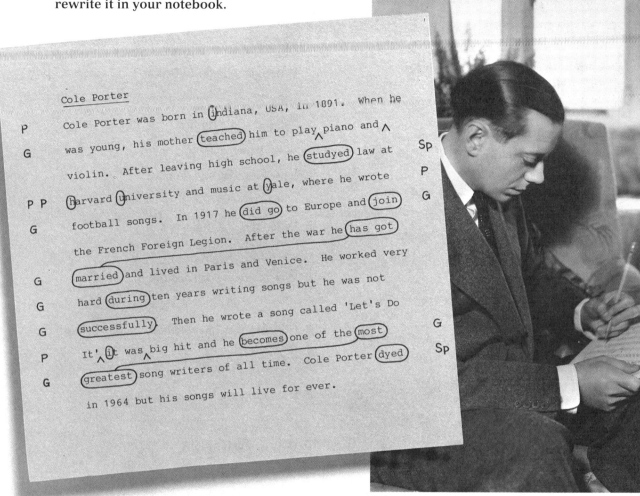

Cole Porter

P   Cole Porter was born in (i)ndiana, USA, in 1891. When he

G   was young, his mother (teached) him to play ∧ piano and ∧   Sp

     violin. After leaving high school, he (studyed) law at   P

P P   (h)arvard (u)niversity and music at (y)ale, where he wrote

G   football songs. In 1917 he (did go) to Europe and (join)   G

     the French Foreign Legion. After the war he (has got)

G   (married) and lived in Paris and Venice. He worked very

G   hard (during) ten years writing songs but he was not

G   (successfully). Then he wrote a song called 'Let's Do   G

P   It' ∧ (i)t was ∧ big hit and he (becomes) one of the (most)   Sp

G   (greatest) song writers of all time. Cole Porter (dyed)

     in 1964 but his songs will live for ever.

4
Join the two sentences using *After . . . ing.*

1 He left high school. He studied law at Harvard University.

   After leaving high school, he studied law at Harvard University.

2 He finished his studies. He went to Europe.

   ....

   ....

3 He left the Foreign Legion. He got married.

   ....

   ....

4 He lived for some time in Paris and Venice. He returned to the USA.

   ....

   ....

5 He wrote songs for ten years. He was still unsuccessful.

   ....

   ....

6 He wrote *Let's Do It.* He became very famous.

   ....

   ....

🎞 *Listening and speechwork 36–40*

LISTENING

1 Listen and choose the best adjective to describe how each person feels.

| happy   angry   frightened |
| excited   depressed |

1 *frightened* ....
2 ....
3 ....
4 ....
5 ....

2 Listen to a radio interview with a paragliding champion and complete the information about her past life.

Name:	Lucy MacSwiney
Age:	....
Started paragliding:	.... ago
First job:	A .... (from 19.......... to 19...........)
First paragliding lesson:	On her .... birthday

PARAGLIDING

WOMEN'S WORLD PARAGLIDING CHAMPION

NAME: Lucy MacSwiney
YEAR: 1989
PLACE: Kossem, Austria
HEIGHT: 13,000 ft
DISTANCE: 15 miles

ORAL EXERCISES

3 Say what's wrong with the clothes.

T: Is it too large?
s: *Yes, it is. Have you got a smaller one?*

1 large – small
2 short – long
3 tight – large
4 expensive – cheap
5 small – large

4 Give rules.

T: Let's park here.
s: *No, we mustn't park here. Look!*

1
PLEASE DON'T PARK HERE.

2
NO EATING OR DRINKING

3
Please do not feed the birds.

4
PLEASE DON'T PICK THE FLOWERS

5
DO NOT WALK ON THE GRASS PLEASE

6
Thank you for not smoking in here.

5 Give instructions in different places.

In a car: drive/fast
s: *Don't drive so fast.*

1 In a car: drive/fast
2 In a classroom: speak/quickly
3 In a park: walk/fast
4 In a choir: sing/loudly
5 In a library: speak/loudly

STRESS

6 Underline the words or syllables which carry the main stress.

1 <u>Did</u> you say <u>five</u> o'clock?
  <u>No</u>, I said <u>six</u> o'clock.

2 Did you say Wednesday?
  No, I said Thursday.

3 Is John coming?
  No, not John, Martha.

4 Are we having the party in Tom's house?
  No, we're having it in your house.

5 Hi! How are you?
  I'm fine. How are you?

6 Don't put it there. Put it here.

Now listen and repeat the sentences. Say the stressed words or syllables as firmly as possible.

PRONUNCIATION

Vowel sounds			
/ʊ/	book	/u:/	boot

7 Listen and tick the sound you hear.

	/ʊ/	/u:/		/ʊ/	/u:/
1	✓	....	5	....	....
2	....	....	6	....	....
3	....	....	7	....	....
4	....	....	8	....	....

8 Repeat the phrases.

I'm cooking some food.
Could you come at noon?
It's a very good book.
Could you put your boots here?

Consonant sounds					
/b/	bet	/v/	vet	/w/	wet

9 Listen and tick which sound you hear.

	/b/	/v/	/w/
1	✓	....	....
2	....	....	....
3	....	....	....
4	....	....	....
5	....	....	....
6	....	....	....
7	....	....	....
8	....	....	....
9	....	....	....
10	....	....	....

10 Listen and repeat the phrases.

It's better and better.
It's wetter and wetter.
He went back to bed.
It was very wet and windy.
The weather was very bad.
I'm playing volleyball tomorrow.

Finale

COMMUNICATION

1 Circle the correct answers.

WOMAN 1: Thanks for a wonderful evening.
I enjoyed it very much.

MAN: It was ¹........

    a) pleasing (b) a pleasure   c) pleasure

WOMAN 2: We enjoyed ²........

    a) to meet you   b) to have met you
c) meeting you

MAN: Have a good trip.

WOMAN 1: Thank you. ³........ you when I get
to Sydney.

    a) I phone   b) I'll phone
c) I'm phoning

MAN: O.K. ⁴........ your taxi.

    a) it is here   b) Is here   c) Here's

WOMAN 2: Bye! ⁵........

    a) Take care!   b) Be careful!
c) You must take care!

GRAMMAR: gerund or infinitive

2 Complete the sentences with the gerund or the infinitive of the verb in brackets.

1 We enjoyed ......*meeting*...... you. (meet)

2 I like .... very much. (swim)

3 There are lots of interesting places

   .... in York. (see)

4 I went to Madrid .... Spanish.
(learn)

5 I hate .... when the
supermarket is crowded. (shop)

6 I've got a lot of homework ....
this evening. (do)

7 I'm very pleased .... you. (see)

8 It was nice of you .... (come)

9 Thank you for .... me. (invite)

10 That's a difficult question ....
(answer)

Blueprint Quiz

**How much can you remember from the book?
Write the answers to these questions.**

1 What is the name *Jorge* in English?

_____

2 What days are the weekend?

_____

3 What language do they speak in Brazil?

_____

4 Which is correct on an envelope: *22, York Road,* or *York Road, 22?*

_____

5 Which is correct at the beginning of a letter: *Dear Mr Birch* or *Dear Adam Birch?*

_____

6 What is the capital of Portugal?

_____

7 On what ocean is California situated?

_____

8 What time do banks open in Britain on Mondays to Fridays?

_____

9 Who was the main film star in *East of Eden?*

_____

10 Who were the Brontë sisters?

_____

11 Where is Disneyworld?

_____

12 What's the weather usually like in Florida?

_____

13 What patterns are bad to wear on TV?

_____

14 What is the opposite of: *He's short and fair?*

_____

15 What date is May Day?

_____

16 What are the comparative and superlative of *good?*

_____

17 What was the first take-away food in Britain?

_____

18 Where is the Great Barrier Reef?

_____

19 If you've got fingers at the end of your hand, what have you got at the end of your feet?

_____

20 Can you smoke in underground stations in Britain?

Pronunciation table

Consonants		Vowels	
symbol	*key word*	*symbol*	*key word*
b	**b**ack	iː	h**e**
d	**d**ay	ɪ	**E**nglish
ð	**th**en	e	b**e**d
dʒ	**J**apan	æ	b**a**d
f	**f**at	ɑː	c**ar**d
g	**g**et	ɒ	n**o**t
h	**h**ot	ɔː	d**oo**r
j	**y**esterday	ʊ	p**u**t
k	**k**ey	uː	f**oo**d
l	**l**amp	ʌ	c**u**t
m	**m**other	ɜː	w**or**k
n	**n**ame	ə	bett**er**
ŋ	si**ng**	eɪ	m**a**ke
p	**p**en	əʊ	n**o**te
r	**r**ed	aɪ	l**igh**t
s	**s**oon	aʊ	n**ow**
ʃ	**sh**e	ɔɪ	b**oy**
t	**t**ea	ɪə	h**ere**
tʃ	**ch**eese	eə	**there**
θ	**th**ank	ʊə	t**our**
v	li**v**e	eɪə	pl**ayer**
w	**w**et	əʊə	l**ower**
x	lo**ch**	aɪə	h**igher**
z	**z**ero	aʊə	t**ower**
ʒ	plea**s**ure	ɔɪə	empl**oyer**

Longman Group UK Limited,
Longman House, Burnt Mill, Harlow,
Essex CM20 2JE, England

First published 1990
Eighth impression 1993

Set in 9^1/$_2$/11 pt Linotype Versailles 55
Produced by Longman Singapore Publishers Pte Ltd
Printed in Singapore

ISBN 0 582 06661 1

Designed by Glynis Edwards
Illustrated by Chris Ryley, Anne Baumn, Kathy Baxendale,
Jerry Collins, Tony Goffe, Maria Manlow, Martin Salisbury,
Dave Simmonds, Carol Wright

ACKNOWLEDGEMENTS

We are grateful to the following for permission to reproduce copyright
material:
BBC Enterprises Ltd for information in the article 'Best of British' by
Mick Cleary in *Radio Times* 2–8 December 1989; Solo Syndication & Literary
Agency Ltd for information in the articles 'Youth Club!' by Peter Higgs in
Mail on Sunday 18th June 1989 & 'Tongues of Money' by Linda Rout in
Daily Mail 8th November 1989; The Sunday Correspondent Ltd for
information in the article 'The Correspondent Questionnaire' in *The Sunday
Correspondent Magazine* 19th November 1989.

We are grateful to the following for permission to reproduce photographs:
Andes Press Agency, page 52 (photo Carlos Reyes); Alastair Black
Photography, page 70; Camera Press, page 13 (photo Gavin Watson); J Allan
Cash Photolibrary, page 28 right; Michael Cole Camerawork, page 21–22;
Bill Cooper/London Contemporary Dance, page 59; Tim Graham Picture Library,
page 6; Hulton-Deutsch Collection, page 71; Longman Photographic Unit,
pages 7, 28 left, 30, 32 above and 40; Mail Newspapers/Solo Syndication,
pages 51 and 72; Scope Features, page 69; South American Pictures, page 1
(Jorge).

Photographs on pages 44 and 66 were taken by John Birdsall, and on page 1
(Adam, Laura, Chris and Sarah) by Con Putbrace.